I0025868

# THE **JAMES BACKHOUSE** LECTURES

This is one of a series of annual lectures which began in 1964 when Australia Yearly Meeting of the Religious Society of Friends was first established.

The lecture is named after James Backhouse, who travelled with his companion George Washington Walker throughout the Australian colonies from 1832 to 1838.

Backhouse and Walker were English Quakers who came to Australia with a particular concern for social justice. Having connections to social reform movements in the early colonies as well as in Britain, Backhouse and Walker planned to record their observations and make recommendations for positive change where needed.

Detailed observations were made of all the prisons and institutions visited by Backhouse and Walker. Their reports, submitted to local as well as British authorities, made recommendations for legislative reform. Many of the changes they initiated resulted in improvements to the health and wellbeing of convicts, Aboriginal people and the general population.

A naturalist and a botanist, James Backhouse is remembered also for his detailed accounts of native vegetation which were later published.

James Backhouse was welcomed by isolated communities and Friends throughout the colonies. He shared with all his concern for social justice and encouraged others in their faith. A number of Quaker meetings began as a result of his visit.

Australian Friends hope that these lectures, which reflect the experiences and ongoing concerns of Friends, may offer fresh insight and be a source of inspiration.

This particular lecture was delivered at The Friends' School, Hobart Tasmania, on 8th July 2019.

Jo Jordan
Presiding Clerk
July 2019

Quakers
AUSTRALIA

# THE **JAMES BACKHOUSE** LECTURES

**2019**
THE **JAMES BACKHOUSE** LECTURE

# Animating freedom:
# Accompanying Indigenous
# struggles for self-determination

JASON MACLEOD

Quakers
AUSTRALIA

© 2019 Religious Society of Friends (Quakers) in Australia
119 Devonshire Street, Surry Hills  NSW  2010
secretary@quakersaustralia.info
quakersaustralia.org.au

ISBN 978-1925231-97-7 (PB); ISBN 978-1925231-98-4 (eBk)

**Design & layout by:**
Interactive Publications, Carindale, Queensland,  Australia

**Front cover art:**
*Animating freedom* by Jason MacLeod and Kym Thomas

# Contents

# About the author

Jason MacLeod has been accompanying the struggle for liberation in West Papua since 1991. An educator, organiser and researcher, Jason works with local communities, campaigns and environmental and social justice movements in Australia, Asia and Oceania. He is a Quaker and descendant of crofters from the Isle of Lewis, Scotland. He lives on Jagera and Turrbal Country and is a member of the Meanjin (Brisbane) Meeting.

# Acknowledgements

I owe a collective debt to the entire Society of Friends in Australia for their faithful support over many years. Accepting the invitation to present this lecture has given me precious space to articulate my framework, something I have wanted to do for years. I also wish to thank a number of people individually. Thank you to Dawn Joyce, Sue Parritt, David Tehr, Mark McLeod, Kerry O'Regan and David Purnell from the Backhouse Lecture Committee for the invitation and to David Purnell for patiently guiding me through the process. Yearly Meeting Secretary Jacque Schultze worked tirelessly behind the scenes to ensure everything went smoothly. I also want to acknowledge David Johnson, Dale Hess, Sieneke Martin, Mark Deasey, Sally O'Wheel, Susannah and Ray Brindle, Gerard Guiton, Sue Ennis and all Friends at the old Northern Suburbs and Toorak Meetings as well as Friends in Tasmania for their early support of my Leading. Without this support, and the tender way it was given at the beginning, it is possible the work would never have taken root.

Thank you to everyone who read the text and offered thoughtful comments. The first draft was nourished by a fruitful dialogue with my long-term friend and colleague, Peter Westoby. Peter's suggestion to read Rilke, and his gentle efforts to nudge me into communicating more deeply, affirmed and supported my attempts to speak from a place of authenticity. Sam La Rocca, Mike and Lesley Storkey, Graeme McLeod, Rosa Moiwend, Dave Andrews, Peter Arndt, Dale Hess, Nathan Dick, Jo Vallentine, Adrian Glamorgan, Robert Burrowes, Brian Martin, Polly (Daksi) Walker, Dawn Joyce, Jessica Morrison and Kerry O'Regan all read drafts, or parts, of the lecture. All offered insightful comments and suggested edits that improved the quality of the text. Thank you to Wendy Monaghan, the Backhouse Lecture editor, who worked on the final edit. My delightful sister-in-law, Kym Thomas, worked with me to design the social cosmology diagram (Figure 6), the movement structures diagram (Figure 8) and the interlocking-circles image that represents my framework (Figures 2, 4, 5, 7, 9 and 11). The image is based on Celtic knots freely available in the public domain. Thank you also to John Waddingham for permission to use his map (Figure 1) and to Peter Westoby and Anthony Kelly for the use of the 'Fanon diagram' (Figure 3), which first appeared in their 2018 book, *Participatory Development Practice: Using Traditional and Contemporary Frameworks*, published by Practical Action.

Of course, the ideas within this book are not mine alone. They were conceived over decades of practice, reflection, reading, dreaming, walking, and sitting idly, and during numerous conversations with people inside West Papua—many with my comrade Biwangko but also with others who are part of Pasifika's wider network. Thank you to all of you. You have sown seeds of fire in my soul. In this regard, I would also like to mention John Rumbiak and Benny Giay. These two elders have been influential in shaping my thinking and helping nurture my own faith and praxis—both nourished by West Papua but taking root in its own soil.

At the end of the day, none of this work would have been possible without the love and support of my immediate family, especially my partner, Manon, and our two boys, Leuca and Emil, and my co-housing buddies: Kerrie, Paulo, Freya and Karlos. As my friends from the Bismark Ramu Group in Papua New Guinea say, may I '*do* thank you'.

Any errors or shortcomings in the text are my responsibility.

# Preface

I first visited West Papua in 1991.[1] That trip changed my life. When I returned to Australia, however, I realised most people had never heard of this nation-in-waiting, even though it was only a swim and a walk away from our most northern border. I suspect this ignorance extends to a large portion of Friends. That is by design. Our imagination has been stopped, denied entry, at the border between Papua New Guinea and West Papua. Ensuring West Papua remains a secret story has been an intentional act by successive foreign governments—including the Australian Government—and their accomplices in the media. This intentional act functions to keep the island divided into two, just as it appears in colonial maps. The result is that the western half of Papua is rendered invisible. I remain shocked by the Australian people's collective ignorance.

---

[1] I use the placenames 'Papua' and 'West Papua' interchangeably to refer to the entire western half of the island of New Guinea, currently occupied by the government of Indonesia. I refer to the Indigenous people of West Papua as 'West Papuans' or 'Papuans', and people of Indonesian heritage as 'migrants'. At the same time, I acknowledge this distinction is not always clear and that many Indonesians are fearlessly standing up in solidarity with West Papuans. At the time of writing, the most impressive of these groups is the *Front Rakyat Indonesia untuk West Papua*, known by its acronym FRI West Papua.

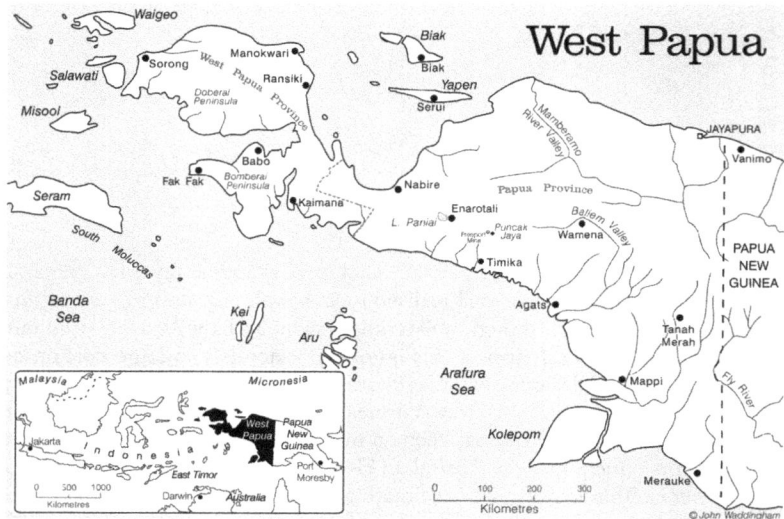

Figure 1: Map of West Papua and neighbouring countries

Back then, the place that was on everyone's lips, especially after the Dili massacre in 1991, was East Timor.[2] I threw myself into that struggle. Many people campaigned against the Australian oil companies Petroz and Woodside, who were cosying up to the Indonesian dictator Suharto to exploit oil and gas reserves in the Timor Sea. We organised sanctuary for Timorese threatened with deportation. We planned nonviolent actions to disrupt the arming and training of the Indonesian military.

When the Timorese voted overwhelmingly for independence in 1999, I decided to renew my original commitment to accompanying West Papuans. After a period of deep reflection, I felt led to make a commitment to accompany the struggle in West Papua for thirty years. But I wanted to do it differently from how I had accompanied East Timorese. My politics needed spiritual roots. I felt called by the Spirit to take the land and people more deeply into my heart. I yearned for my solidarity to be more an expression of love that grows from relationships with people and place than merely a conduit for my politics.

Although my intention was always to support powerful nonviolent campaigns designed to disrupt and ultimately end Australian Government and corporate support for the Indonesian Government's occupation of West

---

[2] Now Timor-Leste.

2

Papua, I was mindful that effective solidarity would only be possible if there were a widespread commitment to, and understanding of, nonviolent strategy inside West Papua and if the nonviolent struggle were being led by Papuans themselves. Australian Quakers saw something in this and agreed to fund my exploration, first as a Donald Groom Peace Fellow and then later with other material and personal contributions. It is something for which I am eternally grateful. Curiosity and relationships slowly grew into a collaboration that is now in its twenty-eighth year. That experience is the subject of this reflection.

––––––––

I feel deeply honoured to be asked to present the 2019 Backhouse Lecture. Quakers are my faith community. It is a tradition that has given me so much. As I prepared this lecture, and the text that accompanies it, I was very mindful that I am among people with profound wisdom and knowledge. I hope I can do justice to your trust in me.

In dialogue with the Backhouse Lecture Committee, we agreed that I would deliberate on my experience of nonviolent solidarity with Indigenous people. Although I have also been immersed in solidarity with Bougainvilleans, East Timorese, Kanaks and First Nation Australians, my deepest and longest engagement has been with West Papuans. In accepting the risk to write—for writing personally about a subject charged with the tears of history is always fraught with pitfalls—I realised I am predominantly speaking to people like me, Quakers who have come from migrant backgrounds. It is my positionality as a fellow Friend, a fifth-generation migrant with mostly Scottish and English heritage and a slightly Queerish white man from a rural working-class background that has shaped these words. I am no expert. West Papuans and Indigenous peoples are the authors of, and experts on, their own lives. Nor do I feel that I have anything particularly new or insightful to say about the practice of nonviolent action or solidarity with Indigenous people.

So, what am I doing?

What follows is my attempt to think, write and speak my way into making sense of accompanying West Papuans in their struggle for self-determination. This lecture is not really about West Papua, much less about West Papuans. It is more a personal reflection on my contribution to animating freedom in the context of historical and continuing colonisation. What I say here is limited: both because it is incomplete and because it reflects just one person's personal practice. By no means should it be considered 'best', or even 'good', practice for what some refer to as 'decolonising solidarity' (Land 2015).[3] Except for a few things, the parts about nonviolence and the presence of a great mystery

[3] See also Pittock 1969, James and Wychel 1991, Brindle 2000, Walker 2006 and Carline 2017 – all Quakers who have also written about colonialism, solidarity and liberation by and with First Nation peoples.

that pervades all things, I am not even sure I can stand on any part of the lecture that follows with the surety and confidence that what I say is true for all times, people and places. It is simply a sketch of my own sense of the terrain at this moment and the journey that has taken me there, leavened with partial glimpses of a greater wholeness seen through the clouds.

Of course, as we Quakers say, I hope that some of my words may also speak to your condition. Mostly, I wish to invite you, the listener and especially Indigenous F/friends, to critique my practice. Collectively, Friends, we need to get better about decolonising our Society and remaking the world.

Although I like to ride my pushbike, fly my paraglider and paddle a boat, at my core I am a pedestrian: a bushwalker, tramper, vagabond rambler. Keeping with that metaphor, this lecture charts how I have sought to navigate the terrain. It contains tales of how I am creating a map, fashioning a compass to guide me, adding my small efforts to our collective labour of undoing colonialism. It is a collection of interconnected vignettes: stories and ideas from a path littered with thorns. I accepted the invitation to present the Backhouse Lecture partly because it offered me a chance to pause. It is a rest stop on an arduous walk, taken sometimes alone, often in the company of others, through dangerous territory: a long walk with an indeterminate destination. You, the audience, are receiving an early and incomplete version of something I am still working out.

Community workers call these kinds of maps 'practice frameworks'. They are ways to organise our thinking in order to direct action (Kelly and Westoby 2018). The framework (Figure 2) I am presenting to you is a collection of the five elements: earth, air, fire, water and spirit, arranged in the shape of the Celtic cross and drawn from the Celtic tradition—wisdom that is found in many other traditions, including the Native American medicine wheel. The elements invite reflection and provide guidance on being grounded and going deeper (earth); vision—seeing far, wide and deeply (air); acting together (fire); holding relationships (water); and sensing mystery at the heart of it all (spirit). Each one is represented by a circle, a significant symbol to both Quakers and First Nation peoples. This lecture is structured around these five elements, book-ended by an Introduction that sets the scene and a conclusion that connects the framework to the state of the Society of Friends in Australia, as I see it. Each element has its own section and every section is preceded by an interlude: a short personal story that provides a starting point for reflection.

Figure 2: My framework: Animating freedom

# Introduction

'The past', as my friends from ELSHAM[4] say, 'has not passed'. It is all around us. It is in people's stories and cut into the landscape.[5] 'Over there,' says Yosepa Alomang, an Amungme older sister, pointing 'there used to be a mountain. It was our grandmother, but foreigners came and dug her insides out.'[6] 'That building', my brother Denny tells me as we walk past it on Jalan Irian in West Papua's capital, 'once housed the West Papuan parliament. It was full of promise. Now it is empty, falling into disrepair.'

Everywhere in West Papua, there are military and police posts. Armed men in uniform, mostly Indonesian, walk the streets, automatic weapons slung over their shoulders. In the markets, migrants sell noodles, rice and consumer goods, while Papuan women sit on hessian mats, selling their produce in the dirt. All these things, and much more, are hourly, daily, weekly reminders of the invasion and ongoing occupation of West Papua.

But the 'past has not passed' not only refers to colonial history. It also concerns history that predates colonisation and how the events in the past play out in the present. Traditional Melanesian society existed before Dutch, Japanese and Indonesian colonisation and although Papuan communities were suddenly and violently disrupted, traditions and traces of diverse Indigenous ways continue. Papuans have held firm to their relationships with nature and ancestors, their ways of living well together, their philosophies and their methods for resolving conflict. When the international community facilitated the Indonesian Government's takeover of West Papua, cultural artefacts may have been burnt, and songs silenced, but not all were permanently erased.

---

[4] ELSHAM stands for *Lembaga Studi dan Advokasi Hak Asasi Manusia di Papua*, the Institute for the Study and Advocacy of Human Rights in West Papua. It was the first and is the oldest Indigenous-run human rights organisation in West Papua.

[5] Papuan theologians draw on Johannes Baptist Metz's articulation of *memoria passionis* to explain the subversive power of these hidden transcripts (Scott 1990): oral stories of violence and oppression experienced at the hands of successive colonial incursions. Giay (2000) describes *memoria passionis* as a kind of 'magma' coursing unseen through the capillaries of the social body (also Giay in MacLeod 2015, 54).

[6] The Amungme are one of the Indigenous custodians of the mountains, forest and rivers, that includes the giant Freeport McMoRan-Rio Tinto gold and copper mine, an enormous hole in the landscape that can be seen from space, and a key driver of conflict.

Remaining Papuan traditions may not always be wholly intact. They may not even be publicly visible. But Papuan ways of knowing, being and doing, continue.

Frantz Fanon, a psychiatrist and revolutionary who was writing at the time of the Algerian uprising against France, gives us analytical tools for understanding and transforming colonial dynamics (Fanon 1963; 1965). Fanon argues that when we think about colonisation we also need to think about decolonisation, about resistance. For Fanon, resistance is not just a loud and defiant 'No!' It is also an assertive 'Yes!'—a commitment to reclaiming personal dignity and creating a new society. Decolonisation is a dynamic, multilayered and ongoing process.

On the side of colonisation, Fanon argues that colonial invasion inevitably gives rise to warfare against the coloniser but also internally, among the colonised. In West Papua, fighting back is not simply a historical curiosity. Papuans have always resisted. And I feel as certain as night gives way to the dawn that as long as the Indonesian Government and its corporate and state allies persist, Papuans will continue to resist. Some resist the Indonesian security forces by engaging in guerrilla war, using modern automatic weapons, stolen or traded with the Indonesians or Papuan kin on one side of the border or another. Others resort to using bows, arrows and spears. Most resist through protests, strikes, boycotts, blockades, occupations and other forms of nonviolent action. They create resistance organisations and nurture their cherished Melanesian culture and identity. Every Papuan I know also practises subtle and persistent forms of everyday resistance: micro refusals to cooperate with oppression and overt and covert ways of maintaining identity. Conflict is also turned inwards. Papuans vigorously argue with each other and occasionally even physically attack one another, triggered by conditions the coloniser has put in place to foment disunity.

Fanon argues that colonisation is not just the process of invasion or the act of dividing and turning people against one another that accompanies a military occupation. Colonisation also includes the process of impoverishing people, weakening their psychic selves and cultivating their dependence on the coloniser. The government and corporations are key actors obviously, but religious organisations, local and international non-government organisations and others providing services also play a prominent role in this. As one Papuan friend once told me, 'If some people raise their voice, the company will come, perhaps even the community development officer and say, "Hey, come into my office, let's talk". They will give that person money or a scholarship or a good job, but usually far away from West Papua.' NGOs, international aid agencies, foreign-government donors and religious organisations collaborate to redirect material support away from resistance and towards livelihood programs and other forms of co-opted economic 'development'. This 'aid' functions to keep a repressive lid on boiling Papuan anger. For the most part, 'development' is designed with a conscious or unconscious neoliberal and neo-colonial agenda.

Colonialism takes many soft forms. Take the recent health crises in Asmat, which many of you will never have heard about. Hundreds of infants and young children died of preventable diseases. It was the end result of frontier migration, of stealing land, cutting down forests and poisoning the river. As a result, quality food—vegetables from gardens, sago and fish—became harder to cultivate or source. Instead of providing quality and equal health care, environmental restoration, access to land or, God forbid, land rights and other forms of self-determination, the Indonesian Government handed out noodles and rice. If this is familiar to you, it is because this is what white power does in Australia. When the response to suffering born of colonisation—in Aboriginal communities or in the prisons that incarcerate people seeking asylum, or elsewhere—is short-term unreflective charity, the coloniser group get to feel good about themselves while avoiding confronting painful questions about the ongoing effects of history and the realities of unequal power and wealth.

While these colonial war practices continue, those facing the brunt of colonial violence are always doing something to change their situation, even when it is insufficient. Resistance *always* occurs alongside colonisation, though it is not always acknowledged or documented by outsiders. Fanon breaks down these imaginative decolonial processes further: into the creation of new organisations, new culture(s), new politics and, ultimately, a new society, depicted in Figure 3. In West Papua, Papuans are not only building new organisations; they are also revitalising and renewing Indigenous traditions. While Indonesian and Western societies demand hierarchical structures, with roles such as chair, secretary and treasurer, and privileges compliance above all else, some Papuans are asking *How have we lived well together in the past? How have other liberation struggles responded to colonialism? What traditional or hybrid forms of organisation might best fit us now, as we struggle in the tiger's mouth?* As the Papuan freedom movement fashions unity, for example, people are wrestling with these questions and tensions. Sometimes these experiments feed into the forging of new cultures and new politics. While not wanting to suggest this is some kind of simple socio-political evolutionary pathway, there *is* a hoped-for trajectory: a new Papua, a free West Papua. Committing to **self-determination** (explained in more detail in the section on water) is the first of five foundational principles that guide how I seek to accompany First Nation peoples' struggles for freedom.

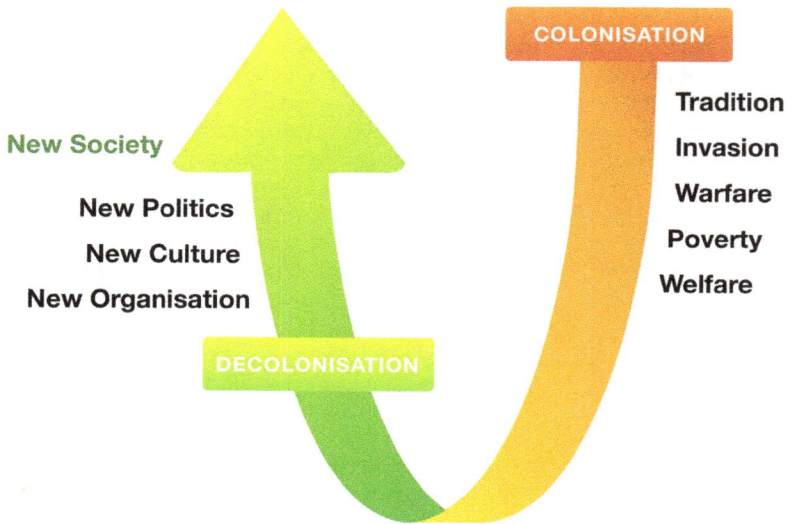

Figure 3: The colonising and decolonising cycle (Fanon in Kelly and Westoby 2018, 46)

What this means in practice for someone like me, besides a commitment to continual education, is that I need to know my place. I never assumed I would do this work; I have been unexpectedly invited into it, and (mostly) I give thanks for that privilege. I am trying to develop my ability to recognise where people are positioned—both individually and collectively—and to carefully calibrate my response to their response (Buber 1937; Kelly and Westoby 2018).

When someone is consumed by anger, raging against the oppressor, it is not the time to collaborate to build a new organisation or to talk about engaging in shared political action. It requires the ability to listen without seeking to argue or soothe. It frequently requires me to have the ability to absorb anger and let that flow through my body without it coalescing into bitterness and settling in my heart (Johnstone and Macy 2012). It often requires me to give space—to work in separate spheres for a while, maybe even for years or decades. This movement between the psychic states of traditional society, invasion, warfare, poverty, and welfare and the building of new organisations, culture, politics and society can be very dynamic. I have been in conversations with Papuan colleagues that have touched on several of these colonial and decolonial crescendos in the space of an hour! It is vital that solidarity workers have a deep understanding of the lively interaction between history and states of being. We need to hone our ability to listen for how history plays out in conversation, listening for these 'codes' that provide clues for understanding people's feelings and how they are playing out in relational dynamics (Freire 1968). Most importantly, we need to take responsibility for addressing the way our own societies and behaviours, projects and good intentions can all be linked to the problem.

As a solidarity worker accompanying the West Papuan movement for freedom, I was immediately presented with at least two big problems. The first and most obvious problem was that I am not Papuan. So, anything that I did needed to be based on a clear **invitation and accountability** to those inviting me. After self-determination, this became the second of five principles guiding the ways in which I accompanied West Papuans in the struggle for freedom. Although I first visited West Papua in 1991, it was not until 2005 that I was asked to directly accompany the freedom movement inside the country. Before that, my focus was on campaigning in Australia, targeting the way my own country exports violence in exchange for resources. Since then I have been asked to accompany the movement as they strengthen unity, co-facilitate a learning dialogue with other liberation struggles and walk alongside people as they deepen their strategy, mobilisation and organising skills. It is what Fanon would broadly call developing 'new culture' and 'new politics'. The next stage will be to lay solid foundations so that Papuans have all the tools, skills and knowledge to manage and lead their own program of activist training and education. Then I will return to strategic solidarity campaigning, channelling my energy to transform the way politics both in Australia and further afield props up the occupation. Since 2013, I have worked with a broad cross-section of the movement. At an organisational level, however, my closest comrade and my co-coordinator is Rosa, a West Papuan woman, also known as Biwangko. Together we work under the auspices of the organisation Pasifika.

Once I had embarked on the more intimate journey of accompanying the movement inside occupied West Papua, this immediately gave rise to the second problem. Those who did not know me were suspicious of me. Why was I doing this work? What was in it for me? Was I a spy working for a foreign government? Was I perhaps funded by one or more transnational mining corporations with a secret agenda to facilitate the exploitation of West Papua's natural resources? Fortunately, the solution to the first problem—the principles of supporting Papuan self-determination, working in relationship with Papuan leaders, and responding only to clear invitations—went a long way to address the problem of suspicion.

However, the principle of invitation and accountability has another important ingredient. In recent years, it has become clearer to me that I should not initiate anything. If I initiate something, it becomes *my* agenda, and that understandably attracts suspicion. It changes the dynamic of cooperation and, if one is not careful, can erode self-belief, self-confidence and dignity among those I work with. But if I listen carefully and I am invited to respond to other people's ideas, to do something together, then it is *their* agenda, the movement's agenda. From time to time, when shared action is enlivened by mutuality, the work becomes *our* agenda. When that happens, it can be magical. That is the elusive space I long to inhabit. I am still honing that skill.

My solidarity work was further refined by third, fourth and fifth principles: **nonpartisanship, noninterference and nonviolent action**. (Lots of *non*s there!) I am partisan to peace with justice and, along with it, committed to decolonisation and self-determination, but I am non-partisan in the sense that I attempt to avoid favouring one group over another and am committed to working with all parts of the freedom movement: young people, older people, women, people from different parts of the country, and people from a cross-section of the groups that constitute the political and social ecology of the West Papuan freedom movement. I am committed to noninterference in the sense that it is not my place to tell Papuans what to do or how to do it. My role is simply to make space for people to learn, to grow in confidence and self-belief, and to deepen trust with one another. I know no better method for doing this than popular and direct education (Lakey 2010).

The fifth principle is **nonviolent action** (also known as civil resistance): action against violence and without violence (Vinthagen 2015).[7] Pasifika is not only committed to imparting skills and knowledge about civil resistance for ethical reasons. We are also convinced, through our own experience and extensive research, that civil resistance inside the country, combined with diplomacy and solidarity outside the country, is the most effective way to animate and win freedom. As a result, we don't support armed struggle in any way. We are, however, willing to work with any person or group, including members of the various armed resistance groups, wishing to explore civil resistance. In Pasifika's view, nonviolent action encompasses the realms of extra-parliamentary action, social movement, cultural resistance, constructive work and everyday resistance.

An understanding of the context of colonisation and decolonisation in West Papua (as informed by Fanon) and the five principles described above—self-determination, invitation and accountability, nonpartisanship, noninterference and civil resistance—are the foundations for my own emerging decolonial practice and Pasifika's work in West Papua. They underpin each of

---

[7] We use the terms 'civil resistance', 'nonviolent action', 'nonviolent resistance' and 'people power' interchangeably. In Indonesian, we use the phrase *perlawanan tanpa kekerasan* (resistance without violence). Civil resistance is further defined in the section on fire.

the five elements in the framework that follows. Taken together and leavened by mystery, their interplay animates freedom.

But first, a story.

# First interlude: Callanish

*Cianalas.* It is a word in Scottish Gaelic that is difficult to render into English. Sometimes translated as 'melancholy', *cianalas* is interpreted by fellow Quaker and Hebridean, Alastair McIntosh (2016), as 'the terribleness of being cut off from one's land and people'. I knew this feeling before I had a name for it, before I even knew my own history. It was the ache in my soul, the hole in my heart: a feeling of not only not belonging but also not being able to belong. It was as if I were hovering above the land: not of it or in it. It was a yearning for something that I knew was missing, but I could never quite put my finger on what it was.

That ache subsided a little when I travelled to West Papua in 1991. As a romantic young person, I found it exhilarating to be drawn into a revolution. As I learnt Indonesian and embarked on shared action for liberation, those feelings intensified. Nearly everything I experienced in those first years of solidarity was intoxicating: people's deep knowledge of who they were; their connection to land and ancestors; vibrant Indigenous cultures; the intense beauty of the mountains, forests and oceans; playful, warm and welcoming friendships. I loved it all. I felt alive in a way I had never before experienced. In a very real sense, I felt I was home … except that I wasn't.

Years later, as relationships matured into greater mutuality, I was gently—but persistently—encouraged to explore my own roots. Papuan friends and colleagues began to ask me more questions about who I was, who my people were and where I came from. Bound up in these questions were others: Why was I drawn to accompanying West Papuans? Why was I willing to risk my freedom for someone else's?

They were questions that gnawed.

Initially, there was little I could tell them except that on my father's side I was from the Hebrides and on my mother's, I was English. I was dimly aware of connections to Poland, and possibly other places, too. But I knew none of my ancestors' stories intimately. I lacked a deep feeling of where I came from and had no pictures in my memory that I could recall, and while, to a certain extent, I was mindful of my privilege, I certainly didn't really consider that colonialism had marred me. Then, in 2016, with funding to attend a peace conference at the University of Bradford, and after a trip to visit Benny

Wenda and his beautiful family, I finally made the journey back to the land of my ancestors.

I arrived in Tarbert on the last ferry. I drove past Amhuinnsuidhe Castle to where the road ends at a remote beach overlooking the diminutive Isle of Scarp. There, in the rain—which had suddenly appeared all around, falling up and sideways as well as down—in the dark, among the mournful sound of sheep bleating close by on the machair, I pitched my tent, grateful that the Scottish 'freedom to roam' allows free camping.

I had only one firm destination: a community centre in Harris, where, according to my Aunty Judy, I might find some answers about where the MacLeods, my family, came from. The following day was a Sunday, which in the deeply Calvinist Harris and Lewis meant everything was closed. (It reminded me of my childhood when shops closed at lunchtime on Saturday and didn't open again until Monday morning. I like to think of this persistent practice as a kind of stubborn Hebridean resistance to capitalism—the commercialisation and materialism—which is colonising our lives.) In any case, I had a day free so decided to drive up to Lewis to visit the famous standing stones of Callanish.

When I stopped to ask directions in Stornoway, I was greeted by a teenager, a fellow MacLeod, who grew up speaking Scottish Gaelic as her first language. Then everywhere I looked—from the Butchers shop to the mechanics—I saw MacLeods. That struck me powerfully. When I finally arrived in Callanish the rain was a constant presence, and I had the stones to myself. They are very impressive, these stones—a little foreboding too. I walked around, gently touching them. I sat and stood in silence, gazing at them from different angles, wondering about the 5,000 years of stories they had witnessed.

Then, without really knowing why, I felt I needed to leave. I didn't know where to go, so I followed something: perhaps it was the spirit of my ancestors, or maybe I heard the voices of the *sìthichean* (the faeries). I ended up on the west coast of Lewis, between the villages of Garenin and Dail Mòr. I walked to the headland and sat on the rocks, were I waited on the edge and stared out to sea, mesmerised by a play of light and diagonal curtains of rain, different kinds of grey and brightness, dancing in ways that blurred ocean and sky. Below and behind me, to the left, just up from a rocky and seaweed-strewn beach, was an abandoned croft, the sad stone ruins of a small hamlet, set against the lush green grass. A couple of sheep grazed close by. I pitched my tent amid the foundations. After a simple meal cooked on my camping stove, I sipped single malt whisky from Skye, read Scottish history and slowly drifted into a deep sleep.

In the morning, I packed up in the rain and then drove back to Harris. At the community centre, an elderly woman greeted me in Gaelic. She telephoned

Bill Lawson, a local historian, and after some discussion and consultation of the old records, Lawson felt reasonably certain that my ancestor, Callum MacLeod (Mhic Leòíd in Scottish Gaelic) was from Dail Mòr (Dalmore in English). The previous night, without consciously knowing it, I had camped a stone's throw from Callum's village. It was entirely possible—almost certain, I think—that Callum visited the very croft where I had pitched my tent the previous night.

Callum and his family were peasant farmers, crofters. In the early 1800s, they would have gathered seaweed from the beach, fished in the ocean, cut peat, grown potatoes and perhaps tended a few cows. When the season was right, they would have hunted and eaten seabirds, *guga* (gannet chicks) and, I like to imagine, gleefully poached fish and deer from the laird's (landowner's) estate. A few generations earlier, the land from the high-water mark to the tops of the mountains would have been collectively owned by the clan, drawn together under the leadership of chiefs. But since the Battle of Culloden in 1746, when restless clans were defeated by the English, the *lairds*, or clan chiefs, fearful of losing their position, shifted from caring about the welfare of their people to hoarding the wealth of their estates. Communal land was privatised and handed over to English colonists or their elite Scottish proxies. In a colonial war practice known as 'the Clearances', Indigenous people—my people—were forced off their land. It was divided up and fenced off to make way for sheep—more profitable than people and less likely to cause trouble.

My ancestors' land was seized by the MacKenzies of Seaforth. Villagers were uprooted, pushed from the fertile machair to drier less-productive parts of the island and then off Lewis altogether in a great migration: an (almost) emptying of the land. The collapse of the global kelp market following the Napoleonic Wars and the potato famine, which spread from Ireland to the Hebrides, intensified people's economic woes and bit deeply into communities' self-confidence, identity and very survival. The historical records show that by around 1850, fifty per cent of Dail Mòr's population had perished. Alcohol abuse and hunger were endemic.

*Cianalas*: not depression, but a deep corrosive homesickness. (Can you hear Fanon in all of this?)

It was in this context that Callum left the village and fled to the slums of Glasgow. A few years later, aided by the Church, Callum migrated, treading a well-worn path travelled by millions of other Scots. Around this time, our name was changed, first from Mhic Leòíd to MacLeod and then finally to the more Anglicised version, McLeod, a spelling that doesn't exist in Lewis.

The effects of these colonial war practices are not only historical. They are ongoing, reverberating through time and space. By the time my grandfather, Alan McLeod was born, Scottish Gaelic was no longer spoken by my immediate family. We no longer knew where we were truly from or who we were. We had lost dances, food and much more. We had become a people uprooted from a bigger story of soil, soul and song. It took many years of work in West Papua before I realised this. Without being conscious of its effect at the time, this profound loss of attachment decentred and disorientated me. It seems a little foolish to write this, but I didn't even know our correct tartan. For years, I thought I was from Skye, not Lewis.

At a collective level, these kinds of distresses and their ongoing effects manifest in emotional and spiritual poverty, addictions and a cultural shallowness: an uncertain vacant space in our collective soul that is easily supplanted by more-dominant and dominating values. Many Scots, for example, were willingly recruited into the services of empire, perpetuating the same kind of colonial violence on other Indigenous peoples as had been meted out on us. In the absence of culture, when language has been lost, when a deeper binding story of who we are fades, when there is no-one who we can call 'our people' and no soil that can hold our affection, what is left? Shopping?

*Cianalas.* The terribleness of being cut off from one's land and people had become a deep collective and individual psychic wound, one that caused immeasurable damage to others and to us. It punctured my soul.

I was finally able to visit Dail Mòr on my last day in Alba (Scotland) in the northern autumn of 2016, when the rain fell softly on the moor. After spending time exploring the archives, talking to Bill Lawson and visiting the MacLeod stone, where I played with my paraglider, I set out to find the village. By the time I arrived in Lewis and turned down the dead-end road to the few scattered identical bleak council houses that now comprise Dail Mòr, it was late at night. I followed the road to the end. Surfers had parked their camper van beside the beach and the cemetery. I left the car headlights on and hopped out. A west wind from the Atlantic was gently blowing ocean spray up the glen. Salt and water on my face, I slowly walked into the cemetery. Rows of headstones gleamed in the headlights. They were nearly all MacLeods. Many of the dead went by the name of Torquil or Torcall, the fourteenth-century founder of clan MacLeod of Lewis.

I slipped into a quiet reverence.

I think perhaps, at that moment, something deep inside me healed.

# Earth: Being grounded and going deeper

Figure 4: My framework: Earth—Being grounded and going deeper

*'Know thyself'*
*– Socrates*

I go deep into the soul of my being to know who I am and why I am being led to do this work. This knowledge grounds me. It energises and motivates me. That is why my visit back to Scotland was so vital. That is why ongoing efforts to trace the stories of my ancestors continue to enliven me. But I am largely guided by feeling here, a different kind of rationality than logic. Before immersing myself in Lewis, I was not even conscious that something within me would connect so profoundly with something in the land and sea of my ancestors.

This work of knowing who we are, where we come from and why we do what we do is foundational. It precedes the 'bonding' talked about by community workers (Kelly and Westoby 2018), and the 'relational meetings' taught by community organisers (Gecan 2004; Ganz 2009). It is a movement inward, downward, and back in time to a 'past that has not passed'.

People long wrested from deep intergenerational attachments to place who wish to animate freedom and accompany First Nation peoples in their struggle for self-determination, I believe, are required to relearn how to see, hear, smell, feel and intuit a longer view of time. Those of us from migrant backgrounds need to think about our own story in terms of generations, perhaps even thousands of years. The task here is to understand where our family is from and how migration has formed us. Can we trace our Indigenous roots back to particular places and ecologies? What is our current relationship to those places and ecologies? In doing so, it becomes possible to reconstruct a bigger, longer, personal intergenerational story, slowly comprehending how the story intersects with the trajectories of colonisation and decolonisation. In what ways have our identities and allegiances changed or been transformed by history: by the forces of conflict, migration, class, race and patriarchy? How were we hurt? What did we lose? What might our ancestors have taken? Whom might they have hurt?

You—I am speaking to other Australian migrants at this point—and I may not have been there for the genesis of colonial violence in Australia. Most likely, we abhor what happened and its ongoing effects. But can we clearly trace—without shrinking into guilt or denial—how our families benefited, and how we continue to benefit, from the systematic creation of inequality, theft and violence meted out to Aboriginal and Torres Strait Islanders? In what ways were we—and our families' beneficiaries—victims, bystanders, perpetrators, resisters, or all of these in different ways? What do we know about the Indigenous people on whose land our family passed through and where we now live? Who are/were your people(s), and what happened to them? What does it take to love a place and defend it as if it were our flesh and blood? What personal work do we need to do so that we, as white folks and/or as forced or voluntary migrants or as people with a refugee experience, arrive in a space where we are as passionately committed to decolonisation as are the Indigenous people?

For a person like me—a relatively privileged white fella trying to figure out how to accompany Indigenous self-determination struggles—unravelling who I am leads me into doing 'shadow work' (as Jungian psychologists would say). And although I have discovered that I too have been wounded by colonialism, the reality is, the world is arranged in ways that make things relatively easy for me (someone who is both white and male). Accepting that reality is hard but ultimately liberating. It helps me think about how to use my privilege ethically.

Sometimes in West Papua, we break open the Bible. In small groups, we 'read the times' and discern what action to take in light of stories of people longing for a better world. I love these kinds of Bible studies. For someone who was once a passionate 'anti-Christian', I have been evangelised by West Papuans (in the best meaning of that word). Sitting on woven mats reading Exodus or the Gospels, my friends in West Papua are energised. Although they see the promise and hope of freedom in those Bible stories, I am depressed. People like me are more aligned with the Pharaohs than with Moses. But as a student of social movements and revolutions, I know that Moses and the disciples need allies, people from within the structures of power who are prepared to become accomplices in transforming violence and rebuilding a gentler world that is kinder for all of us. This is a path away from guilt and towards enlightened self-interest.

To the extent that this work is deeply relational, long-term commitment is required. Yes, it is possible to do short stints of decent work in a professional capacity with Indigenous people, work that can contribute to undoing, resisting or renegotiating colonialism. I have had that experience a few times. Years ago, I was invited to work with my dear friend Sam La Rocca to co-facilitate a Green–Black dialogue between traditional owners and conservation groups around shared goals of caring for country. Sam had been asked to facilitate conversations between environmental groups and representatives of the Murray Lower Darling Rivers Indigenous Nations alliance of Aboriginal Nations (MLDRIN). The chair of MLDRIN had asked Sam to facilitate conversations on country with different Indigenous nations, and Sam invited me to join him. My involvement was only two short weeks. I think I did a good job. But that was only possible because there were people holding the space, anchored in long-term commitment. I would like to say that the long-term commitment included all the environmental groups that we worked with, but I am not convinced that, as organisations, many of them 'got it'. Maybe we expected too much of environmental groups. First Nations have soul and a lot of 'skin in the game'. In contrast, organisations have missions, campaigns, and policies and procedures, and they have leadership with varied levels of commitment to self-determination. It is a profound mismatch.

At some point, I realised that as an individual I needed to make a long-term commitment. Back in 1999 when I told Biwangko that I would made a commitment to accompany the struggle in West Papua for thirty years, I was feeling pretty chuffed with myself. Her response brought me back to earth: 'Why only thirty years?' she asked. I wasn't expecting that. Biwangko embodies a different view of time.

Now, twenty-eight years into my journey of accompaniment, I understand that a commitment to place and people is not something I can pick up and put down like a hobby, especially when it concerns Indigenous peoples and their struggle for self-determination. I think about my ancestors in the cemetery on the beach at Dail Mòr. I wonder if I honour them and the land that holds them. Deep in my bones, I pray that my friends in West Papua won't lose any more of their land, their languages, their cultures. I pray they will never know the stony soul-eating coldness of *cianalas*.

# Second interlude: The 1,000-drum canoe

My Papuan friends speak of their island as bird—a beautiful bird of paradise—green and blue, lightly brushed with the white of snow-capped peaks, resting just above Australia. In the west, the bird's head looks towards the Indonesian archipelago. Stretched out behind the bird's body, a long luxuriant tail flows east to Papua New Guinea. In conversation, song and imagery, the bird is never cut in half. The bird of paradise in my friends' imaginations conforms to both geography and culture. It is whole and wholly alive.

This idea of one land, one ground, one people, one soul—from Sorong in the bird's head to the island of Samarai at the tip of the bird's tail—is a recurring vision. The Free Papua Movement, or Organisasi Papua Merdeka, has both a bird, the majestic crowned pigeon, and the words 'one people, one soul' adorning its coat of arms. Thomas Wainggai, a well-known Papuan nationalist who died in jail, dreamt of a Melanesian federation stretching from West Papua to the Solomon Islands and beyond. Before Wainggai, Arnold Ap, a Papuan musician and anthropologist, and his colleague Eddy Mofu, who were tortured then mutilated by the Indonesian military, united land and culture in song.

For ordinary people straddling this imaginary straight line on a map, the border regularly recedes out of view. Villagers of Wutung, for instance, have their homes on one side of the border and their food gardens on the other. The Ok people from the rugged Star Mountains and their highland neighbours, the Muyu/Yonggom, conduct their affairs—hunting, gardening, trading and marriage—on both sides of the border. When the Malind Anim, whose land stretches across the southern savannah—replete with eucalyptus trees, huge termite mounds, kangaroos and crocodiles, much like northern Australia—play their mighty hourglass drums, they echo in the gulf country of Papua New Guinea.

The land, and the creatures that dwell in the earth, water and sky, confer no respect to the fantasies of empires. Mighty forces of nature regularly move the border one way or the other. The Fly River, which marks the southern political boundary between Papua New Guinea and West Papua, mocks the vagaries of geopolitics. It breaks it banks every time it floods, throwing its snaking coils one way, then the other, shifting to the demands of unstoppable flowing water, pouring down from New Guinea's central mountain spine.

The ancestors, the land, the birds, the animals and the Papuan people pay no homage, no tribute and no allegiance to maps ruled up in The Hague, Jakarta and Canberra. Just as the nation of Poland maintained its integrity even as it disappeared from maps for over 100 years, the nation of West Papua, and the larger Melanesian and Pacific family knows who it is, even when others fail to acknowledge it. An undivided land (and sea) is a deeper lived reality despite the fact the bird and its people are cut and caged. As my friend Airileke Ingram says, 'Melanesians of West Papua and Papua New Guinea didn't cross the border, the border crossed us.'

Airileke Ingram and Benny Wenda, a West Papuan leader, captured this feeling in a song they wrote together, 'Sorong Samarai'. It goes like this:

### Sorong Samarai

Light up the fire… let that fire burn…

#### Verse 1

Rize up freedom fighter
Rize up and take your stance again
Bird of paradise never die in vain
Melanesia yumi rize up again
For all who live in darkness
can see the great light afar,
dawn of a new day come
with the Rize of the Morning Star.

Seagull calling like in a Yolngu dream…
Song to claim the land and sea (ooh yeh).
Sorong Samarai one people
One soul one destiny

#### Chorus

Sorong Samarai
One people one soul
One destiny
Sorong Samarai
We gotta keep on pushing forward

Sorong Samarai
One people one soul
One destiny
Sorong Samarai
One people one soul
One destiny

One, one, one, one,
Wa, wa, wa, wa…
One people one soul one destiny.

**Verse 2**

One man one kundu
Satu orang, satu tifa
Suara nenek moyang kita
Papua Tana kami
Get your weapon of choice
Come back again
Like an east coast boomerang
Wamena to Biak
Serui, Manokwari
Timika, Merauke, Jayapura
Sorong Samarai x 2

**Chorus**

Papua Merdeka
Papua Merdeka
Papua Merdeka
Papua Merdeka
Papua Merdeka
Papua Merdeka
Papua Merdeka
Papua Merdeka

My organisation, Pasifika, and my Papuan co-conspirator, Biwangko, worked with Airileke, Ronny Kareni, (another Papuan) and other friends from Papua New Guinea, West Papua and Jamaica to turn that anthem into a music video. When Biwangko and Airileke travelled to Biak Island in the north to film the video, they met Denis Koibur, a Biak *koner* (prophet).

Denis was once a university lecturer teaching anthropology. Now he is a song man and mystic. Denis was enthralled by Airileke and Benny's audible vision of a land united from Sorong and Samarai. He was amazed that Airileke was a drummer, a Papua New Guinean from a village called

Drum Drum, Gabagaba in Airileke's Motuan tok ples (language). Denis told Biwangko that the ancestors had visited him in his dreams and foreshadowed her and Airileke's coming. He spoke of four drums—in the east, west, north and south—awakening a spiritual movement that would heal the island.

Denis is no idle dreamer. He may be a mystic and an artist who speaks in allegory and poetry, but he is also a man of action. So, when the ancestors told him in a dream to build an ancient Byak canoe, a *wairon*, the likes of which had not been seen in nearly 100 years, he obeyed.

As Quakers, we recognise that inconvenient impulse.

When Airileke and Biwangko met Denis, he and Swandibru, the small group of people around him, had all but finished building the *Wairon*,[8] a huge canoe. Denis asked us to help him finish the canoe and then sail it and its cargo of 1,000 drums from Sorong to Samarai in a moving ceremony: a journey to heal the land, restore culture and reunite east with west.

It wasn't a question of 'should we do this?' All of us were drawn in by cosmological forces beyond our control. Like Denis, we simply obeyed.

The canoe was finished, and Denis and the crew sailed to Samarai.

The bird quivered. And, some of us felt it.

---

[8] The *Wairon* is both the name of a type of Byak canoe and the name of the actual canoe that Denis, Rosa and others sailed to Samarai, Papua New Guinea.

# Air: Vision

Figure 5: My framework: Air—Vision

Denis, and the *Swandibru* group of which he is a part, have vision. The soulfulness and authenticity of that vision animated Denis and others to do things that they never imagined themselves doing. It set in motion ripples that cannot be contained. Denis never mentions the word 'freedom', but his thinking and his language reverberate with the sound of it. That is why, as co-coordinators of Pasifika, Biwangko and I were willing to dash our budget on the rocks to ensure the *Wairon* remained afloat, because without a vision, the people, like Alice, are lost like a rudderless boat adrift on an endless ocean.

But what does our vision of freedom, or *gutpela sindaun* (the good life) as they say in Papua New Guinea, look like? What is its shape? Its contours? Its texture?

To animate freedom, you need a big enough, deep enough and wide enough dream to hold different people's various concerns, desires, and understandings of freedom. In West Papua, freedom is translated as *merdeka*.

The meaning of that word is deep and varied (MacLeod 2015, 86–107). But sometimes the vision of *merdeka* gets hollowed out, translated into its most limited form: an independent state. The danger of this shallow interpretation is that it obscures the deep and destructive nature of both colonial violence and structural violence embedded in the state. Such violence, among other things, includes colonising Papuans' minds, shaping them to think and act as Indonesians, and to have faith in an extractive economy that is ubiquitous, like cancer. If a new state is achieved without thoroughly contemplating the consequences of dependence on the giant Freeport mine, for example, or without safeguarding communal land ownership or without deeply valuing the richness of Indigenous place-based identities or without thinking through how entwined the modern state is with empire (and many other things), then Papuans might get independence but it could be without freedom.

That is why Denis Koibur's vision energised us. It was a vision grounded in a place-based Papuan cosmology but one that reached out to other Melanesians on both sides of the border and charted a trajectory towards other possibilities. All of us who long for liberation, I think, need big stories, big visions of freedom, but ones that are not totalising, that allow the particular to flourish in their own diverse beauties (Escobar 2017). There is a vital connection here between vision, analysis and design. If vision is a compass, then analysis is the map. We can't really know where we should go unless we truly understand where we are. Charting those possibilities is the place of imaginative, careful and experimental design, deeply attuned to justice, place and the earth (Escobar 2017).

So what kind of 'map' and 'design work' might breathe life into locally grounded and enlarged visions of freedom? One of my mentors, the practitioner–scholar and nonviolence maverick Robert Burrowes (1996) writes about social cosmology. I find his framework extremely helpful, for understanding both where human society is now and the direction/s we need to move in. Burrowes writes that four interconnected components make up a society's social cosmology: (i) its particular pattern of matter–energy use (how we relate to the material world and use energy); (ii) its social relations; (iii) its prevailing philosophies, including a conception of human nature; and (iv) its strategies for dealing with conflict (Burrowes 1996, 1). All four of these components are mutually reinforcing. A society's philosophy, often expressed through a set of spiritual, religious or ideological beliefs, for example, determines how it relates to the material world and energy, organises that society to live well together and resolves conflict.

The world's dominant social cosmology—although it has different shapes and hues in different places—is, in a word, 'empire'. It has given rise to the multifaceted crises that we now find ourselves in. Empire's relationship to matter–energy is based on non-renewable sources. Governments and their

26

corporate masters' extractive relationship to natural (and human) resources mirror the dominant view of nature as lifeless things, only valuable when consumed. Empire's social relations are imperial and capitalist and shaped by racism, classism and sexism. Its underlying philosophies privilege logic to the exclusion of other rationalities, like *eros* and *mythos* (McIntosh 2001; 2016). In economics, empire stresses constant material growth. In politics and ontology, it is shaped by hierarchy and individualism, buttressed by the belief that human beings are selfish, competitive and aggressive. Empire's strategies for dealing with conflict range from the use of the law, which is not equipped to address structural violence, to military operations designed to protect and extend privilege for the one per cent. This is the social cosmology that has delivered widespread inequality, war and a climate that is no longer safe for human beings and other life.

In contrast, people like Denis and the Swandibru group point towards a social cosmology that embraces the use of renewable energy; nurtures social relations or ways of living well together that are based in equality and that recognise human beings *are* nature; values structures that are non-hierarchical and highly participatory; encourages communal ownership; appreciates the holiness and interconnectedness of all life; embraces a view of human nature that is not set in stone, but one that recognises its variability; and uses dialogue, exchange and ritual, and other nonviolent means to resolve conflict. It is a social cosmology and a way of being that existed in Melanesia before colonisation. In many villages in New Guinea, this view of the world remains a vibrant living foundation for living well together.

Think for a moment of other fragments of hidden histories that also point to these other worlds—different from empire—worlds that refuse to go away. I am sure that many of you reading this are involved in aspects of this cosmological work. Such aspects include intentional communities, cooperatives, community-owned renewable power, permaculture, participatory budgets, nonviolent action, and promotion of ideas like universal basic income (Wright 2010). The movement from the dominant cosmology towards localised expressions of 'the good life' embrace the twin goals of constructing justice *and* obstructing injustice. Some movements, like the Zapatistas in Chiapas, Mexico, and the Landless Workers' Movement (*Movimento dos Trabalhadores Rurais Sem Terra*, MST) in Brazil embrace both resistance and the creation of people-centred and environmentally just alternatives, what Gandhi (1945) called 'the constructive program'. All these examples are significant, even if they are still insufficient, not fully integrated and not yet at a scale to be globally transformative. What Robert Burrowes does is unify these ideas within a coherent conceptual framework. If we are to find our way out of this mess, then we need to intentionally develop all four parts of the social cosmology at the same time. Out of this soil, the 'good life' will flourish, expressed differently in different places. It is the promise of what Martin Luther King Junior called the 'beloved community' and what Gandhi (1909) called 'Hind Swaraj'. It is Arturo Escobar's 'pluriverse' (2017). In Melanesia, it is simply 'the village'. If the element of earth brings us back and down, air moves us forward and up.

Pasifika supported the song 'Sorong Samarai' and the journey of the *Wairon* because they touched on some of these components, particularly on an underlying philosophy and a view of social relations that moved away from empire towards a deep understanding of *merdeka* and *gutpela sindaun* that resonated in West Papua and Papua New Guinea. It is for the same reason that Pasifika is now supporting food and gardening. When we talk about food, we touch land. When one talks about land, this not only raises questions about resources and the extractive economy that is a raison d'être for the occupation; it also starts a conversation about Indigenous governance systems. At the same time, the practice of shifting from a staple diet of rice and noodles to sweet potatoes and sago, for example, will begin to lay the foundation for an organised mass withdrawal from dependency on the Indonesian state and colonial economy. And with that will come the possibility of a general strike as well as the firm but gentle assertion of dignified Indigenous identities.

Ideological 'purity', which rules different political, social and economic initiatives 'in' or 'out', is much less important than the directional flow away from empire and towards 'the good life'.[9] In the case of strategies for dealing with conflict, for instance, I am not looking to collaborate with 'perfect' activists who have already embraced nonviolence in all aspects of their life. What is much more important to me is to work with people who are enthusiastic about exploring resistance. From a position of validating the need to resist, it becomes more possible to deeply explore different kinds of resistance, what it might take to make these different approaches work, the value in or problems of combining approaches, and the consequences of different types of resistance. That is equally true for the other components of the social cosmology. When discerning whom to work with, it is the direction, pace and willingness to move together and the kinds of values and behaviours that animate people that matters most to me, not 'correct thinking'.

---

[9] I am indebted to *Chris D. Brown* for this insight. Chris wrote his PhD thesis about the possibility of nonviolent revolution among the Naxalites in India. I also want to acknowledge one of my long-term mentors, Dave Andrews, who speaks of 'open-centred' and 'closed-centred' modes of thinking, reminding us that what matters most is not what we believe or what group we belong to but whether we are moving towards love.

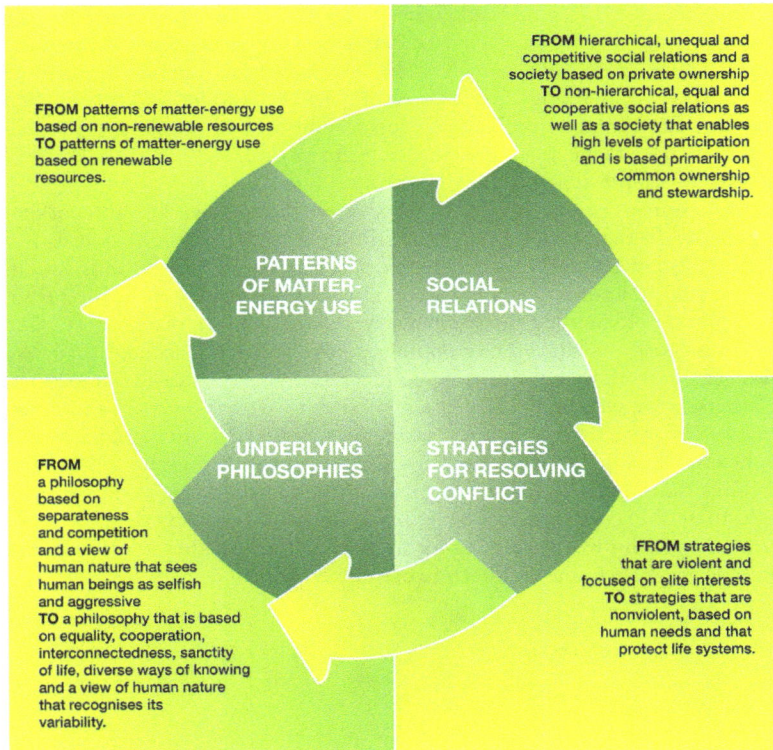

Figure 6: The four mutually reinforcing elements of a society's social cosmology and directional flows away from the dominant cosmology of empire towards freedom and the 'good life'. Adapted from Burrowes (1996, 1–3). Designed by Jason MacLeod and Kym Thomas.

As a solidarity worker, I am listening for how and when the dream of a nonviolent society aligns with the dreams of the West Papuans I am accompanying. That alignment is often partial. What is important is that the specific activities and larger programs we are working on contribute to integrated, Indigenous cosmological visions of 'the good life'. The dreams that spark collective action arrive in many different forms. For instance, they may come as visits from the ancestors, such as the ones received by Denis.

To even begin to understand, I need to nurture my ability to become a cosmological boundary walker, alive to wisdom contained in conversations, stories, voices, myths, images and other forms of cultural expression. These are Freirean codes that are an important foundation for participatory community work (Freire 1968; Kelly and Westoby 2018). Dreams can also be sparked by exceptions, memories and stories of what once existed, a time when the problem was not a problem. Visions can also be as simple as a people's determination to be free. This is the realm of imagination —of desire— kindled by irrepressible hope.

Of course, there is incredible creative tension in this. We are working for the world that we long for while still living with the world as it is. For the nonviolent resister, it is problematic to waste this one precious life on radical goals that enjoy little support and have no hope of ever bearing fruit. In addition to fomenting (nonviolent) revolution, there is a place for pursuing reformist goals, which can buy oppressed communities space and time. We also need to work with the existing political realities, structures and processes. Conversely, we will never enjoy 'the good life' if we don't invest in the varied features of prefigurative politics, economics and social and ecological life, right now, 'building the road as we walk it' (Horton and Freire 1990). That requires radical action and having faith that the impossible is possible. To hold these things in tension I try to have one eye on the next step, the other on a 500-year horizon, searching for ways to channel weather into cracks and hairline fractures in the architecture of empire.

# Third interlude: Yambi

In November 2005, I received an unexpected invitation to attend a clandestine meeting of West Papuan resistance leaders in Yambi, Lae, Papua New Guinea.

Those present spanned the spectrum of West Papuan society: church leaders, ex-political prisoners, women, youth and student activists, and members of the *Tentara Pembebasan Nasional* (TPN) or Free West Papua Movement National Liberation Army, a loose grouping of guerrilla fighters waging a low-level armed struggle against the Indonesian state. Also present were a number of West Papuan leaders from the diaspora. A Papua New Guinean pastor, who led prayers each morning and evening, and I were the only people present who were not from West Papua. I had been invited by members of what was then called the West Papua Peace Task Force, a group of human rights defenders who had turned their attention to the work of unifying the independence movement and nurturing the transition from armed to unarmed struggle.

Members of the Peace Task Force asked me to give a presentation about some of the relevant lessons from other nonviolent struggles and to speak about the kind of nonviolent strategies and tactics that could be employed in the West Papuan context. The West Papuan organisers of the meeting felt that the Indigenous people in West Papua were facing 'slow-motion genocide'. This, combined with the fact that men who had spent more than thirty years fighting Indonesian forces in the jungles and mountains of West Papua would be present at the meeting, along with a number of ex-political prisoners who had spent long periods in jail, meant it was an invitation I felt somewhat nervous about.

As I rose to deliver my presentation, I took a deep breath. I acknowledged the traditional custodians of the land we were staying on. I acknowledged the sweat and tears of those in the room, the sacrifices made by people who have since passed on. In formal Indonesian, I thanked the organisers for the invitation, and then with all the courage I could muster, I told those present, 'I don't support independence.'

You could have heard a pin drop. This was a meeting of independence activists and resistance leaders. Many had spent years in jail for their political beliefs. A number were hardcore jungle fighters. To my left was Richard Yoweni, the leader of the TPN north-coast faction. I don't think I will ever forget his intense gaze on me at that moment. Kelly Kwalik, the legendary guerrilla leader killed by Indonesian troops in December 2009, had sent a representative, who, with bushy beard and dreadlocks, was sitting directly in front and eyeing me suspiciously.

'I am an outsider,' I continued. 'It is not my role to campaign for independence. It is up to you as Melanesians living in the land of your ancestors. And while I am committed to standing in solidarity with you in the pursuit of peace with justice, ultimately it would not be Australians like me who would pay the political costs for campaigning for independence. It will be people like you. For me as an outsider, to argue for independence would be to assume a colonial mantle. I have no right as someone who is other-than-Papuan to presume that I can speak on behalf of what you as West Papuans want. Instead,' I went on to say, 'I am committed to accompanying you on your journey.'

The subtle difference between self-determination and independence, and what I offered to share about what West Papuans could learn from other nonviolent liberation movements must have been valued because later my friends from the Peace Task Force invited me to work with them on an ongoing program of nonviolent training and education. The discussion resulted in a plan, which over time has become the basis for Pasifika, the organisation I founded to support the work and which I now run with my colleagues Biwangko, Vivian, Ladonna, Moyu and Nathan.

# Water: Relationships

Figure 7: My framework: Water — Relationships

*'I will give you a talisman. Whenever you are in doubt, or when the self becomes too much with you, apply the following test. Recall the face of the poorest and the weakest man [person] whom you may have seen, and ask yourself, if the step you contemplate is going to be of any use to him [her/them]. Will he [she/they] gain anything by it? Will it restore him [her/them] to a control over his [her/their] own life and destiny? In other words, will it lead to swaraj [freedom] for the hungry and spiritually starving millions? Then you will find your doubts and your self melt away.'*
*– Mohandas K. Gandhi (1948)*

Relationships are at the heart of all forms of community work. That is equally true for my work accompanying freedom in West Papua. But as an Australian man invited to work across cultures, languages, places and race—who is from a nation founded on the notion of white supremacy—my relationships with the West Papuan freedom movement and West Papuans are complex. I suspect that complexity may be true for any collaboration between insiders and outsiders connected to the same cause. For me, this movement in and out of different relational spaces includes working as a professional with clear boundaries, acting as an unpaid solidarity activist sharing goals, being a friend, and being embraced as kin and family. Among other things, it includes behaviours like keeping quiet; knowing when to talk; 'staying in my lane' as some put it, which is important when being the only person in the room who is other-than-Papuan; being invited to hold space as a trusted and 'objective' facilitator; sharing wealth; and sometimes vigorously disagreeing in spaces where criticism is neither invited nor welcomed but concerns matters in which I have a vested interest, including my own wellbeing and safety. It is the constant challenge of how to use unearned privilege ethically. Sometimes I get that right. Most of the time, it feels like a dance by an awkward white guy who is not great at feeling the music. That is a bit what it felt like in Yambi. Sarah Banks calls it 'ethics-work' (Banks 2019): no rules, no codes, no cookbook.

Earlier, I touched on some of the principles and practices that guide relational solidarity work. It is as easy and difficult as embodying respect (Sennett 2002). The three most important of these principles and practices are self-determination, invitation and accountability. This is what anchors me. It could easily be the subject of this entire lecture.

As stated earlier, during the story from Yambi, there is a subtle but important difference between 'self-determination' and 'independence'. 'Self-determination', I have written previously, 'exists as an ideal, process, and outcome' (MacLeod 2015, 32). As an ideal, self-determination refers to the realisation of the collective aspirations of Indigenous peoples living within defined cultural, linguistic and geographic territories and the ability of those peoples and groups to participate fully in the decisions that affect their lives. As a process, self-determination refers to the difficult, contested and ongoing practice of securing, maintaining and fulfilling desires for political, economic, social, and cultural rights that affect people's and groups' abilities to determine their own future. This requires ongoing struggle, one that does not end with attaining a cherished political goal (Scheiner 2006). As an outcome, self-determination refers to the claim to the right of self-government within the boundaries of a given territory. That may include independence or it may not. In West Papua, self-determination includes Papuans' participation in a referendum over the territory's political status, but it is not limited by this. More-localised demands for self-determination can be translated into demands for greater administrative and legislative rule; local Indigenous control over land and resources; the ability to define and direct development activity, including the right to say no to development; exercising control over migration;, subjecting the security forces to civilian control, including the development and enforcement of stringent human rights mechanisms and laws; and the freedom to express distinct cultural and religious identities. Support for self-determination —as an ideal, process and outcome— is about aligning Pasifika's agenda with Indigenous and community-led visions and strategies, entwined with the pursuit of real and tangible benefits for the host community.

Accompanying Papuan-led self-determination agendas (informed by Smith [1999] and others) is impossible without bonded and trusting relationships. But to engage in mass-based action, which is essential to animate freedom, requires some kind of 'vessel' able to hold relationships and guide action in a coordinated and disciplined way. This is the realm of structure, creating strong but flexible enough containers to hold the work.

At one end of the spectrum is the work of helping to form, and accompanying, small and informal groups. In the middle of the spectrum is the painful challenge of maintaining an organisational base. In this story of work, that middle space is mostly where Pasifika is working. The organisational base needs enough solidity to strengthen movement capacity (and keep our funding) but also enough flexibility to respond to the demands of a movement for self-determination, which is being hammered by a violent state and rapacious corporations. At the other end of the spectrum is what community workers call 'meta-level work' (Kelly and Westoby 2018): seeding and maintaining coalitions, alliances and federations.

As movements try to go to scale, it is the horizontal social infrastructure that matters most. In a place like West Papua, the biggest challenge that the movement faces is repression. As nonviolent leaders have risen up, the state has consistently cut them down. Arnold Ap, Thomas Wainggai, Theys Eluay and others were all killed when they stepped up and built mass support. Hierarchies are particularly vulnerable to repression. When the Indonesian Special Forces allegedly assassinated Theys Eluay in 2001, the organisation Eluay led, the *Presidium Dewan Papua* (Papuan Presidium Council), collapsed.

On the other end of the organisational spectrum are loose networks. Networks are certainly more resilient to repression. Their flexibility also means they are much better at tactical innovation than are hierarchies. However, they lack the ability of hierarchies to coordinate and direct large numbers of people.

One way to combine the strengths of coordination that hierarchies possess with the resilience and creativity of networks is to form decentralised network structures. These kinds of structures are governed by collective leadership unified by vision, strategy and a shared narrative and brand. They set out to find and nurture local leaders and support them to build groups and grow other leaders, who then form other groups. In this way, a movement can spread rapidly, with a reach into all parts of the country. Examples include *Otpor!* in Serbia, the National Council of Timorese Resistance in East Timor, the United Democratic Front and the Coalition of South African Trade Unions in South Africa during the apartheid struggle, and the Kanak and Socialist National Liberation Front (FLNKS) in Kanaky (New Caledonia).

A recent experiment to form distributed network structures in West Papua came out of the meeting in Yambi. Those present at the meeting decided to form the West Papua National Coalition for Liberation (WPNCL). The WPNCL then became one of the three founding coalitions of an even more expansive umbrella structure: the United Liberation Movement for West Papua (ULMWP).

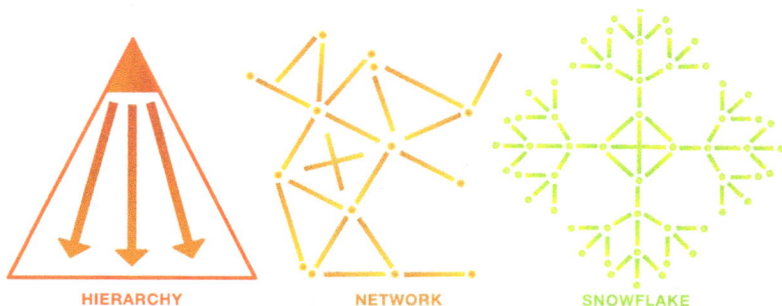

Figure 8: Three different types of social movement structures

The evidence from the field of civil resistance is clear. Distributed network structures perform better when it comes to organising leaders, mobilising for mass action, resisting repression, maintaining unity and achieving goals. A further and difficult challenge in West Papua is the inside–outside dynamic between the Papuan diaspora and the movement inside the country. The engine of change is inside West Papua. That is where the power and legitimacy of the movement lies. The challenges inside West Papua include limited political space, a lack of resources, and difficulties in communicating and moving around the country. At the same time, the role of the diaspora is vital. They are the ones who are able to travel more freely and engage in diplomacy. As a movement, we are still collectively trying to figure out how to build a functional, effective and resilient movement structure that can function well inside *and* outside the country, while nurturing unity and acting strategically.

# Fourth interlude: Bringing West Papua back to the family

Frank Bainimarama, the Fijian autocrat, is not a friend of West Papua. Throughout the six-month campaign for West Papua to become a member of the Melanesian Spearhead Group (MSG), he courted the Indonesian Government and blocked the West Papuan leadership at every turn, from beginning to end. So, when Bainimarama stood up to address West Papuan leaders Octo Mote and Benny Wenda, I was not prepared for what he was about to say.

It was June 2015. My comrades and I had slipped into the exclusive meeting room of Honiara's Heritage Park Hotel. Inside the room were the heads of state and foreign ministers of four of the members of the MSG: Vanuatu, Papua New Guinea, the Solomon Islands and Fiji. Also present were representatives of the fifth full member of the MSG, the Kanak and Socialist National Liberation Front, or FLNKS, a coalition of political groups from Kanaky, more commonly known as New Caledonia, struggling for independence from France. Observing the meeting were a large delegation representing the Indonesian Government and, of course, the West Papuans. For the first time ever, the two countries, Indonesia and West Papua—one officially recognised, the other stepping out from the shadows—sat beside each other as equals.

The previous night, Manasseh Sogavare, then Prime Minister of the Solomon Islands, announced that the ULMWP would be accepted as a member of the MSG. We had won. Officially, the ULMWP was granted observer status, but it was membership nonetheless. The Pacific Island leaders also decided to grant the Indonesian Government associate membership. It may not have been everything the movement wanted, but it was a giant step forward. This subregional forum, often overlooked in international affairs, suddenly became a permanent setting for dialogue on West Papua's political status.

Back in the Heritage Park Hotel, the formal close of the meeting was beginning. Octo Mote had just addressed the members of the MSG. And the

Indonesian Government's Deputy Minister for Foreign Affairs had tersely replied. Now the five members all had a chance to speak.

It was Bainimarama's turn. 'You have brought West Papua back to the family', he said.

I couldn't believe it. This was the ULMWP's campaign slogan. We had come up with this phrase at a meeting I facilitated in Brisbane, with the West Papuan leadership and allies from the Pacific. It was the way we had framed what we wanted. This prayer, and demand, was taken up across the Pacific.

Previously an enemy, Bainimarama now addressed the West Papuans as kin.

# Fire: Nonviolent collective action

Figure 9: My framework: Fire—Nonviolent collective action

*'With one hand we say to the oppressor. 'Stop what you are doing. I refuse to honor the role you are choosing to play. I refuse to obey you. I refuse to cooperate with your demands. I refuse to build the walls and the bombs. I refuse to pay for the guns. With this hand I will even interfere with the wrong you are doing. I want to disrupt the easy pattern of your life.' But then the advocate of nonviolence raises the other hand. It is raised outstretched—maybe with love and sympathy, maybe not— but always outstretched with the message that… 'No, you are not the other; and no, I am not the other. No one is the other…' With this hand we say, 'I won't let go of you or cast you out of the human race. I have faith that you can make a better choice than you are making now, and I'll be here when you are ready. Like it or not, we are part of one another."*
*– Pam McAlister on Barbara Deming (McAlister 1988, 6-7)*

The fourth element in my framework for animating freedom and standing with people struggling for decolonisation is fire. Fire represents action, specifically collective nonviolent action. It is the work of Deming's 'two hands of nonviolence': one dedicated to resistance, the other to (re)constructing better worlds. There are many stories to tell, but the one introduced in the fourth interlude, about the campaign to secure West Papua's membership of the MSG, is historically significant. It also illuminates the multidimensional dynamics of nonviolent resistance.

———

Fifty years ago, academic Judith Stiehm (1968) observed that the phenomena of nonviolent action existed on a spectrum, with principled behaviour on one end, pragmatic action on the other. This was an old debate in nonviolent action circles. Nonviolence as ethics or nonviolence as strategy? Gandhi on one side, Gene Sharp on the other. But it is a false dichotomy.

Quakers have fallen into this trap from time to time. We have embraced our lofty principles and Testimonies. We tell ourselves that it doesn't matter if we are only a few, so long as the world doesn't change us. There is value in that stance. But as a code for a lifetime of activism, it can become lazy. Worse, it can portray a sense of hopelessness, that deep down we don't really believe change is possible. For people steeped in privilege this attitude is not good enough. At times, we have failed to think like hard-headed strategists. At other times, the spirit of neoliberalism has seduced us into a clueless retreat into individualism. But individual ethical purity is of little succour to people like West Papuans who don't desire to live permanently at the pointy end of violent exploitation.

In 2015, my colleague and comrade Stellan Vinthagen wrote a book in which he observes that nonviolent action comprises not two dimensions but four: strategy, ethics, dialogue, and prefigurative politics. In doing so, Vinthagen was returning to a deep reading of a decolonial Gandhi informed by sociology. Vinthagen argues that when each of these four dimensions are brought together and held in creative tension, they release a transformative force more powerful than any bullet or bomb.

It is by no means a perfect example, but the campaign to bring West Papua back to the Pacific family, which the previous story points to, used all four dimensions intentionally and, I believe, to great effect. What follows is a brief description illustrating how those four dimensions played out in the campaign. Taken together and enlivened by some of the other dimensions mentioned previously, most notably the energies of air and water, this reading of civil resistance informs movement/meta-level work.

———

*Dialogue.* When Bainimarama welcomed the ULMWP into the MSG, it was the conclusion of a protracted and difficult dialogue. In this campaign, one aspect of that dialogue was between political elites—among the foreign ministers and heads of state of Papua New Guinea, Fiji, Vanuatu and the

Solomon Islands, and the FLNKS. These were closed and, to some extent, hidden spaces: decision-making meetings that West Papuans were locked out of (Lukes 1974; Gaventa 2006). Peace builders refer to elite negotiations like these as 'track one' dialogue. But although the campaign to bring West Papua back to the family ultimately compelled Jakarta to sit at the same table with West Papua, where they faced each other as equals, the most important dialogue in this campaign was not within the five permanent members of the MSG or even track two dialogue between mid-level civil-society leaders but internally in West Papua, within the grassroots freedom movement (track three dialogue). The ULMWP, the coalition of three large alliances of resistance groups inside West Papua, did not fall from the sky. It was built on the foundations of long-term relationships and efforts. It was nurtured. Many people played essential roles, all contributing to building a shared consensus around the need to unify the movement. But the most vibrant gardeners, those labouring in the field of *merdeka*, I believe—as someone who, together with Biwangko, had a front-row seat observing the process over many years—were young people inside West Papua.

When I first began this work, I did not fully grasp the extent to which ego, factionalism and disunity had restrained and undermined West Papuans' power (remember the Frantz Fanon wisdom from the Introduction). In the beginning, I did not think about the relationship between what we were doing and the dream of building social power. Many of the early workshops on nonviolence were with individual identity- and interest-based groups such as church leaders, women, students and particular resistance groups.[10] That continued until my comrades Sam La Rocca and Karina Nolan and I met Forkorus Yaboisembut. At the time, he was President of the National Federal Republic of West Papua. Yaboisembut was the one who requested the meeting. This was just before he and his colleagues were imprisoned for holding an open-air mass meeting to discuss independence, upon which the police and military opened fire, killing five. Our meeting also took place before he fell out of favour with both his own group and the wider movement.

Yaboisembut had heard of the workshops we were running. He wanted to meet us and interrogate our methods. He told us the workshops were helping. He had watched the videos on civil resistance that my colleagues and I had arranged to have translated. Then he asked us to do something. It was a request that would have profound consequences, not only for us but also for Yaboisembut.

'The central and recurring problem in the movement' Yaboisembut emphasised, 'is disunity'. He explained that although the workshops had made space to share skills and knowledge about civil resistance, they needed

---

[10] Other forms of practice include action learning, action research, facilitation, brokering resources, and organising campaigns of nonviolent action.

to contribute more to the process of building unity. They needed to be undertaken by outsiders who were trusted by all the groups. Yaboisembut was asking us to abandon training and education with individual identity groups and resistance organisations, and instead to work with mixed groups, with participants from different places with different persuasions and different identities. The practice of unity and of movement-orientated nonpartisanship is 'going to be hard for you', he said, 'but I want you to do it.' It was wise advice.

For the next five years, Pasifika did just that. Guided by the wisdom of John Paul Lederach (1995, 38–55), my colleagues and I decided to partly focus on working with young people who were mid-level leaders. They were aged between twenty and forty, and were close to senior resistance leaders. They were also connected to the grassroots and were committed to them growing in power. I would like to tell you we had a plan and that the work was guided by deep analysis and good design, but in reality, this decision was more intuitive. We were feeling our way carefully in the dark rather than clearly seeing where we were going. Bringing people together across geographic, political, class, race and gender fractures certainly made the workshops more conflictual. Two things in particular helped. First, we recognised conflict as a generative force (Francis 2002). Second, we integrated Arnold Mindell's (1995) concept of 'mainstreams and margins' into the pedagogical process, making space to notice difference and diversity while seeking to build expansive, inclusive, robust and shared movement norms.

Over time, key youth leaders from different resistance groups, who trusted one another and shared an analysis, put pressure on elders/leaders from the three largest political coalitions inside the country to agree to attend a meeting whose purpose was to form a larger, more-inclusive umbrella organisation. That coalition, the ULMWP, was finally formed at a meeting in Vanuatu held during November and December 2014, three years after our meeting with Yaboisembut.11 At every stage, when senior leaders started to push for their own group to dominate, young people intervened, reminding their elders to think of the whole. The crucial role of young people and these diverse grassroots mid-level leaders remains invaluable but still not fully appreciated.

———

*Strategy.* I support dialogue (tracks one, two and three), especially in the case of shared action for a just peace. Sooner or later, people from opposing sides need to sit down and talk to one another. There will be no just and sustainable peace in West Papua without some kind of political negotiation,

---

[11] Biwangko and I were part of the team that facilitated that meeting. Also present was Rev. Francois Pihaatae, Aisake Casimira, and Murray Isimeli from the Pacific Conference of Churches.

ideally with those most affected—West Papuans—having the most to say, backed up by trusted international third parties. One side has to take the first step. West Papuans have done that, even agreeing to a unilateral ceasefire. The Papuans held that ceasefire for several years in the hope that Papuan-led efforts to push for talks between Jakarta and Papua, mediated by a third party, may bear fruit. They may need to take the initiative to talk again, but for now, 'dialogue' has become a dirty word in West Papua. It has been poisoned by the bitterness of being ignored by Jakarta. My friend and mentor, the Rev. Dr Benny Giay, describes this as like 'boiling a stone that never cooks'. Likewise, in South Africa, young people are saying, 'no more dialogue, we have demands!' They recognise that dialogue between grassroots groups and political and economic elites often ends as a form of co-option by the powerful.

Dialogue is one dimension of civil resistance. But perhaps the dimension that civil resistance is best known for, is mass action. Large numbers of people pour into the streets, unarmed, refusing to back down. To do collective action well, movements need a strategy. Campaign and movement strategy utilise the rationality of logic. Among other things, effective collective action requires long-term goals, shorter-term SMART objective/s,[12] primary and secondary targets, a plan for getting from 'A' to 'B', a set of tactics that can be escalated over time, a collection of allies who support key movement goals and campaign objectives, and an analysis that guides it all (see, for instance, Burrowes 1996; MacLeod and Whelan 2015; Lakey 2018).

To become members of the MSG, West Papuans needed to win the support of at least three of the five permanent members. We knew that Vanuatu and the FLNKS supported the movement. Over the course of the campaign, it became clear that Fiji and Papua New Guinea were in the pockets of the Indonesian Government. It was unclear, however, where the Solomon Islands Government stood. Therefore, outside West Papua, the focus was on persuading the Solomon Islands Prime Minister, Manasseh Sogavare, and his cabinet to support the ULMWP's application to become a member. That strategy had both a high-level diplomatic component and a grassroots component. Both components focused on shifting opinion in Honiara, the capital of the Solomon Islands. In the last month of the campaign, we had more than 140 positive news stories (more than 5 per day) in the Solomon Islands alone.

Inside West Papua, the strategy was to delegitimise the Indonesian Government's occupation of West Papua while simultaneously demonstrating widespread support for the ULMWP. The strategy relied on one core tactic: a paper petition. The only problem was that the Indonesian state considered, and still considers, support for the ULMWP as tantamount to sedition. But

---

[12] An acronym for specific and strategic (you will be closer to your long-term goal if you achieve it), measurable, achievable (can be done), realistic (within the capacity of the group) and timebound.

that was no deterrent to Papuan activists. Organisers with the ULMWP travelled the length and breadth of West Papua—by ship, plane and car and on foot—to collect more than 55,000 signatures from all of West Papua's seven regions. The petition not only included the names, addresses and signatures of the petitioners, but people's state-issued identification cards were also copied and included as further proof of authenticity. In addition to radical pro-independence Papuans, many Indonesian migrants also signed. Those who could not sign their name supplied a fingerprint. In addition, West Papuan leaders from all the mainline churches signed letters of support. So too did the National Council of Customary Chiefs in West Papua (or DAP, *Dewan Adat Papua*), women and student groups, Papuan intellectuals, armed guerrillas, and civil servants and politicians working for the Indonesian Government.

During the signature-raising campaign, which took place between March and May 2015, Indonesian security forces shot dead 32-year-old Obangma Giban, a village chief from Yahukimo (MacLeod 2015). In May, a month before the MSG meeting in Honiara was due to take place, 487 activists were arrested for participating in the campaign. Some of them were tortured. Officers from the Mobile Police Brigade (Brimob) in Manokwari, part of a national Indonesian paramilitary police force, stubbed out cigarettes on Alexander Nekenem's body while the head of the Manokwari Regional Police, Tommy H Pontororing, denied Nekenem and his compatriots access to lawyers. Police also demolished communication posts at places like Cendrawasih University, where people could go to sign the petitions. Countless scores were savagely beaten, including many of my friends.

It was clear that the ULMWP campaign was having an effect when the Indonesian President travelled to West Papua to elicit the support of the two governors to oppose the ULMWP. In a stunning act of noncooperation, Lukas Enembe, the Governor of Papua Province, switched off his phone for three days and failed to meet the President.

———

*Ethics and the constructive program.* Vinthagen calls this third element of his framework 'normative regulation'. Norms are the non-formal and often unwritten 'rules' of expected behaviour of groups and people in various social situations. Normativity may be codified in legislation, but norms are different from laws. Norms include etiquette, rituals, traditions and cultural practices that members of groups—small and large—are socialised into through participation in daily life. Over time, these norms become internalised; they regulate behaviour and belonging, and they influence group members' motives and habits. All groups, communities and societies have norms. This is one of the features that help bind people together and, in some cases, keep people apart. However, the normative worlds of people, even those from the same group, may look fundamentally different from one another.

Nonviolent activists simultaneously uphold some norms while criticising and even breaking others. For example, the civil rights activists who campaigned for equal rights in the United States claimed norms of equality, taking responsibility for one's actions, and not harming others in word and deed. At the same time, however, these activists criticised and broke widely held social norms such as obeying authorities. Through training and participation in the movement, fearlessness was cultivated. Social behaviour previously abhorred, such as being arrested and serving time in jail, became reframed as badges of honour. This was true for not only the civil rights movement but also the Indian independence movement and many others. Normative action is also about creating the new nonviolent society and embodying that with our lives, social interactions, group processes and new institutions, even though our goals of a just and sustainable peace are yet to be fully realised. Gandhi called this the 'constructive program'. To the extent it is become a parallel form of a nationwide decision making inside and outside West Papua, the formation of the ULMWP is one example of the West Papuans' constructive program.

The training and education work that Pasifika have been undertaking in West Papua is, in part, a contribution to developing norms of disciplined nonviolent action and organised mass participation. Many people have been part of that work. When we began in 2005, civil resistance was not at all understood and rarely practised, even though there is a hidden history of nonviolent resistance that predates Gandhi (MacLeod 2013). During the course of the petition, it was clear that had changed. Papuans carried out a range of fearless nonviolent actions. They maintained discipline in the face of arrests, beatings, torture and even murder by the Indonesian security forces. What was most evident was their self-belief and confidence. The pride people felt in unifying in the face of corrosive colonialism was electrifying.

———

*Utopian enactment.* Finally, civil resistance can be understood as prefigurative politics, an unfolding political drama and a willingness to persist—recognising the power of sacrifice to inspire and mobilise. Vinthagen calls this *utopian enactment.* Many Friends will be uncomfortable with this, but in a context of entrenched structural injustice where an unarmed movement is pitted against an extremely ruthless opponent, it is important that 'goodies' and 'baddies' are clearly identified. The moderate and nonviolent action of the movement needs to be clearly differentiated from the violence and cruelty of the opponent. Activists' willingness to voluntarily endure suffering for their cause is one of the things that move ordinary people to participate in nonviolent action. That is one reason why discipline is so important. Civil resistance is divisive and deliberately so (Engler and Engler 2016, 197–223). But as fellow Quaker George Lakey (2001) is fond of saying, it is 'a sword that heals'. Being able to positively polarise a situation in order to compel people to choose a side but then being able equally as quickly to depolarise a situation in order to enable healing and reconciliation is difficult. But it is exactly what nonviolent movements excel in (Engler and Engler 2016).

In the 'Bring West Papua Back to the Family' MSG campaign, we sought to act in ways 'as if' West Papua was already part of the Pacific family. We were seeking to activate a decades-old history that had been forgotten: when the Pacific had actively embraced West Papuans as kin.[13] The best way to do that was through emotional and dramatic communication. We used face-to-face interactions, cultural diplomacy, relationship building, music, animation, posters, stickers, and social and mainstream media to move people's hearts, particularly in the Solomon Islands. It was a strategy that ultimately worked, evidenced perhaps most clearly by Bainimarama's comments in Honiara.

---

[13] Papuan church leaders Reverend Kabel and Reverend Maloali of the Evangelical Christian Church were present at the founding of the Pacific Conference of Churches in 1961 at the Malua Theological Seminary in Samoa. Papuan politicians Marcus Kaisiepo and Nicolas Jouwe were present at the founding of the South Pacific Commission (SPC), a forerunner to the Pacific Island Forum. The SPC was established by six countries, including Australia and New Zealand, in 1947. Its founding charter is known as the Canberra Agreement. This is history remembered by West Papuans and forgotten by many Australians, particularly federal politicians.

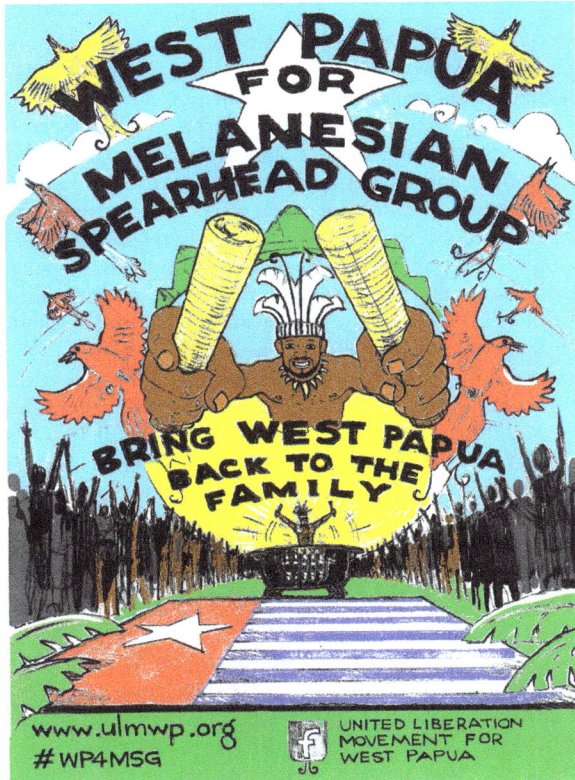

Figure 10: The Bring West Papua Back to the Family 2015 campaign poster
Credit: Designed and drawn by Michael Kumnick based on conversations
facilitated by Pasifika with ULMWP leaders, solidarity activists, and
community leaders from Oceania

———

As activists and Quakers, we need to develop our skills and experience
in order to simultaneously develop all four dimensions —dialogue, normative
action, strategy and utopian enactment— holding each in creative tension, each
one complementing another. The synergy results in more-powerful nonviolent
action and the possibility of more coordinated collective action. Strategy

builds the possibility of dialogue, negotiations and treaties. Normative action strengthens capacity within the movement to generate alternatives. At the same time, normative action creates a basis for a parallel system, which assists a strategy that is designed to undermine the power of the opponent. Utopian enactment engages with emotions, transforms enemy images and initiates discursive change. Normative action confronts, resists or transforms the ways in which emotions and images might block transformation of the conflict by posing attractive visions at the centre of the conflict. It simultaneously paints visions for the creation of new norms and possible alternative ways of living. Dialogue builds the foundations of people power, which is strategic nonviolent action, and coordinates the activities of the three other dimensions. Dialogue also contributes to changing the conversation about the problem, drawing on normative action and utopian enactment to do so.

Over time, this approach has informed what I think of as 'meta-organising'. My colleagues and I from Pasifika try to analyse the entire conflict system as it interacts across three domains: inside West Papua, inside Indonesia and in the international community. That analysis is an ongoing, iterative and dialogical process. Based on this dynamic analysis, grounded in the five principles, and guided by the five dimensions, we carefully and tentatively make interventions designed to alter the atmospherics of the conflict 'field'. Each one is an experiment, undertaken in the context of invitation and accountable relationships. These interventions may be as simple as a conversation or as large as hosting an international meeting. Each intervention is carefully monitored and evaluated. This requires extreme flexibility. (Fortunately, Melanesia is a place that hones one's ability to respond flexibly to a constantly changing environment!) The long-term goals underpinning our interventions are threefold: to achieve particular campaign objectives, build movement power, and change the political weather. Because we might be wrong, we are rigorously committed to a nonviolent ethic. I accept there is a touch of boldness here, which is why it is important to intervene cautiously. At worst, we want to do as little damage as possible.

# Fifth interlude: The breadfruit tree

I first went to West Papua in 1991. Feeling restless and dissatisfied with university, I had dropped out of Law School. Then I had dropped out of an Arts degree. It had been a series of progressive 'picnics', disrupting formal education in order to learn. I hitched a ride north to Cairns and made my way to Papua New Guinea in search of adventure. I walked the Kokoda track, climbed Mount Wilhelm and then walked back down to Madang on the coast before catching a light aircraft to the headwaters of the Ramu River. I landed on a remote airstrip on the upper reaches of the Ramu River and walked to the headwaters of the Keram River, a tributary of the Sepik. There I negotiated to buy a dugout canoe. The head of a *puk-puk* (crocodile) was carved on its prow. My paddle told the story of the village.

For several weeks, I slowly drifted downstream, progressively improving my paddling technique. By day, crocodiles would surface beside the canoe. Flocks of hornbills flew overhead, the deafening beating of their wings sounding like a fleet of helicopters. At night, I would pull into villages nestled in the jungle and sago swamps. Sometimes I would stay for a few days, sometimes just a night.

Three weeks into my journey down the Keram, I arrived in Bunam village. It was Saturday. The family I was staying with asked me to attend church with them the following morning. At that time, I was unable to distinguish between Christ and the Church. I was a committed anti-Christian, appalled by the hypocrisy of the imperial Church, the infighting among denominations and the disregard some in the Church had for local cultural beliefs and practices. Partly out of respect for my hosts but mostly because I felt like I could not refuse, I said I would go to church.

It was not to be. That night I awoke with a throbbing headache. My head felt as though it were about to explode, and pain shot down my spine. A severe fever had taken hold of me, and I was in no position to go anywhere. As night slowly turned to dawn and the village began to stir, the family I was staying with showed me to the village headman's house where I could rest. Within half an hour, I vomited and then fell unconscious. For three days, I lay racked with fever, slipping in and out of consciousness.

Miraculously, I had fallen ill just thirty minutes' walk from one of the three health clinics located along the more than 600 kilometres of the Keram River. People from Bunam village carried me to neighbouring Kevim village, where the local health workers, Chris and Marilyn Mangon from Simbu, literally saved my life. Here were a people who, in the eyes of the materialistic West, had nothing. For the most part, folks lived a subsistence life. And yet they had given me life itself! Then, when I left, Chris and Marilyn gave me gifts! It was an experience I will never forget. And in the process, I incurred a debt to the hospitality and generosity of Melanesian people (and humanity) that can never be repaid.

After three days, I regained consciousness. When I was well enough to walk, the first thing I did was go outside. Now, I am not one for visions. I had never had a vision before, and I have not had one since. But there, in Kevim village, on the edge of the forest by the banks of the Keram River I had what I can only describe as a mystical experience. When I walked out of the house where I had spent a week recovering, my spirit was immediately drawn to a breadfruit tree on the edge of the village. Instead of seeing the outer form of the tree, I saw its living heart. A stream of light was flowing through the tree into the ground, linking earth, tree, river, sky, sun and village into one seamless flow of pulsating light. I knew then, with certainty, with a kind of knowing that lodged deep inside me, that the interconnectedness and holiness of all life was no fanciful idea: it was a living and constant reality. And I had seen it!

I hauled myself up into that tree. I hugged the trunk tight. I cried like a baby. The local people thought I had totally lost my mind! They gently pulled me down and took me fishing.

My original plan had been to travel the world in search of ever-wilder experiences. I would travel around the world searching for and consuming one new experience after another. But as I looked around me, that idea no longer made any sense. The Mangons and the people of Bunam village had given me my life back. They asked nothing in return. Then, when I was leaving the village to continue my way by canoe to Angoram, they had given me gifts. I was utterly overwhelmed.

In an instant, everything came into focus for me. The only choice that made sense was to give back to society, to embrace the web of holy relational reciprocity, to joyfully attempt to fulfil obligations that I could never repay, and to attempt to do so with a sense of irrepressible gratitude. I decided I would return home, curious and excited about figuring out what it meant to serve others and life itself.

In that moment, in the boughs of the breadfruit tree, I experienced an abiding sense of what I think may be the deepest possible form of solidarity: unity with the whole of life. Inside me, I knew God is love. All is sacred. Everything, to paraphrase Jon Muir, is tethered to everything else.[14]

[14] Jon Muir (1838-1914) was a Scot who emigrated to the United States. He was a writer, explorer, mountaineer and scientist, whose passion for wild places and sense of responsibility to protect them helped create the world's first national park in the Yosemite Valley.

# The fifth element: Spirit and mystery

Figure 11: My framework: The fifth element — Spirituality and mystery

*'May you awaken to the Mystery...'*
*– John O'Donohue*

As Quakers, we believe there is something of God in all people. Some of us go further. We proclaim there is also something of God in all things, even breadfruit trees. Even rocks. All life is holy. Everything is interconnected. That has been my experience, stamped indelibly on my soul during that first trip to New Guinea.

This is not pantheism but pan*en*theism, a belief in a universal spirit of love abiding in all things, within and beyond the universe: the cosmic Christ. The practice of panentheism takes me back to nature, back to wild places: the open sky, mountains, forests, rivers, oceans. There, I am stilled by awe.

The experience of a kind and friendly universe—a feeling of unifying love and belonging—is profoundly liberating. It is an encounter with the Divine. At a deeper level, beyond my ability to consciously articulate it and in spite of the evidence to the contrary, I have a feeling that everything is going to be okay, that death is not the final answer. In its place is constant transformation, a universal movement towards love. Of course, I don't always reside in this space. Like you, I rage and cry at injustice and cruelty. But beyond grief is a sense of being held, which I have felt not just once but again and again. Remembering this enables me to regularly step out of fear, even if only momentarily. Practising this more consciously and intentionally makes it more possible to share risk in the walk towards freedom and unity.

Encounters with the pulsing heart of life concerns inner work: prayer, meditation and personal growth. There is also a collective dimension. This is all about making space to go deeper together. It involves the deliberate use of ritual, attention to group dynamics, use of framing to alter the wider psychosocial context, and a shift of focus from problem-saturated conversations to narratives that privilege the skills and knowledge of how people survive, resist, and hold on to hope. It is life as a stilled presence, full of awe, a state of collective union.

Everyone Biwangko and I work with in West Papua has known the buds of tears that spring from trauma. Every day, West Papuans experience pain caused by the sting of racism. Many of the scars of colonial violence are present when Papuans gather together; they mar people's bodies and show up in their behaviours. In workshops and meetings, we use rituals like *hadir* (present).[15] We evoke the names of those who have passed on in the struggle for *merdeka*, who have been disappeared, or who might be in jail. We bring their memory and presence into the room by calling out their names and responding '*hadir*'. At the end, we ask, 'How long are they with us?' (*Untuk berapa lama dorang hadir?*) We all respond, 'For always. For always. For always.' (*Untuk selamanya. Untuk selamanya. Untuk selamanya.*) These kinds of rituals, and practices such as Bible studies based on contextual and liberation theology, are interventions in group work that bring awareness into the room of a God who yearns for justice, who grieves with us. They are therapeutic without straying into therapy. The work of making space to encounter Spirit also includes efforts to alter the wider 'field'—the collective socio-psychological dynamics that operate at different levels—and shape what people believe about the problem and what they believe is possible. The 'Bring West Papua Back to the Family' communication strategy that I shared earlier, for instance, was designed to alter the political weather in this way and to intervene internally in people's collective imagination of what may be possible. At a technical level, this is about the use of 'collective action frames', but for those of us who have faith it is much more. It is a kind of spiritual midwifery.

To be honest with you, this dimension of my framework is the least developed. I still lack the precise words to describe what is going on or even to articulate what I am doing. I am a novice trying to figure out how to work intentionally with various energies at play, to give my work more depth. I long to hone my ability to make a more welcoming space for the Spirit so that the groups I work with and the collective action that we and they undertake are less formulaic, more infused with soulfulness and love. Having said that, as an apprentice 'alchemist' or *sanguma* (*suangi* in Indonesian)—one who is able to

<hr>

[15] I learnt this from Salvadorian friends who were involved with the Base Christian Communities in Central America in the 1980s who opposed an authoritarian and repressive government that had backing from the United States. In Spanish, this ritual is known as *presenté*.

shape and direct energy—I feel that I am on the way.[16]

Twenty-eight years since first starting my journey down the track—on the far side of the Highland Clearances—I am rediscovering a more expansive version of who I am. On a good day, I go forth in gratitude (Johnston and Macy 2012).

---

[16] *Sanguma* is a *Tok Pisin* word. In English, it is often translated as 'sorcerer' or 'witch doctor', but I think a more accurate translation is 'energy worker', 'mystic' or 'spirit-conscious community worker'.

# Conclusion

In this lecture, I have attempted to articulate my own (emerging) framework. Animating freedom encompasses five interrelated dimensions: being grounded in knowing myself and a deeper story of why I am called to do this work (earth); seeing far, wide and deep (air); holding relationships and structuring social movement (water); taking nonviolent collective action (fire); and encountering mystery (S/spirit). Underpinning these five elements are five principles: self-determination, invitation and accountability, nonpartisanship, noninterference, and nonviolence/civil resistance. For most of the last twenty-eight years, this work has been focused on strengthening strategic capacity inside West Papua. But the intention has always been to confront and change the way the Australian Government and corporations prop up the occupation. This kind of solidarity work is happening, but more slowly than I anticipated.

As I wrote in the preface, this framework guides me. It is a map and compass, which has been fashioned while navigating the terrain, in the company of and in dialogue with West Papuans themselves. It is one way in which I make sense of the work. It is a frame for helping me choose what to do *and* what not to do. Within each element are other sub-dimensions, principles and tools. For reasons of time, however, I have concentrated on what is at the core of my framework. At the same time, the framework is dynamic, not static. I am constantly developing it as I grow and as the work and the context changes. I am trying to open myself to being continually educated by those I am in relationships with and those who challenge me.

The framework described within this lecture is the fruit of nearly thirty years' work. But what if you are just beginning, just setting out on a decolonial journey? After all, we all start somewhere. I am reluctant to offer a checklist at this point because I don't feel there is a formula or set of rules to follow, let alone check boxes to tick off. This is soul work. It looks different for different people. But I do have some questions, offered in the spirit of *Advices and Queries*:

- Who are you?
- Where are you from?
- In what ways does your story, and a longer story of your family, intersect with colonialism and empire?

- As you come to know those stories, what feelings arise in you?
- How are you taking responsibility for the legacy of your family's history?
- How are you ethically using your own privilege?
- What places hold your affection and how are you nourishing that?
- What does 'showing up'—being in relationship with Indigenous people—look like for you?
- What does it mean to 'hold back', 'be silent', 'keep your ego in check' and share your wealth and resources with Indigenous peoples working for self-determination?
- What steps are you taking away from empire and towards 'the good life'?
- In what ways are you cultivating space, within and without, so that your journey is increasingly taken in the company of others?
- In these dying times, how are you living life as a joyful obligation, animated by love?

For me, a most helpful behaviour and attitude in all of this has been cultivating respectful curiosity. But I still regularly get it wrong. We all do. None of us is perfect, including those we are accompanying; therefore, nourishing an ethic of care for ourselves and for one another is part of the walk.

What, if anything, might this mean for Friends as a whole, particularly Friends in Australia and other places where the colonial project is alive and well—around and within us—even when we are clueless of its presence? Although there is deep resonance between my framework and our Testimonies, I don't know the answer to that. Beyond stimulating—or perhaps agitating—a few individuals, this lecture and these words might not travel far. However, I have observed two things in particular that I wish to share with Friends as a whole, particularly Friends in Australia. I say these things as one of us and in gratitude to a Society that has made it possible for me to animate my leadings. I am going to risk being bold here, partly because 'the microphone' is in my hands and partly because I have a feeling that embedded in my own personal journey is something universal that might speak to our condition as a whole Society.

The first observation concerns the individual. As Quakers, the primacy of the conscience, the desire to hear and respond to the 'still small voice', the sovereignty of the individual, if you like, is at the heart of our faith and practice. It is what has shaped our Testimonies. It is not easy to listen to the 'still small voice'. There is the cacophony in our heads, a fear of being powerful, and a multitude of entanglements that distract and domesticate. They obscure the possibility of movement from 'empire' to a 'good life'—for all of us. To the extent that the majority of us can escape these snares and are able to listen and respond authentically to the Spirit, we are enlivened as Meetings and as a Society.

The problem is that our faith and practice is in danger of being co-opted by the shadow side of the wider society and these dying times that we find ourselves in. Freire named that malignant spirit as 'neoliberal fatalism', a sense that 'broader change is not possible' (Paulo Freire quoted in Denborough 2008, x). I think a key feature of this 'stuckness' is individualism, nurtured by ignorance, isolation and powerlessness—that we have no value and no purpose aside from being consumers. As Quakers, we have potent spiritual tools to address these blocks to transformation, but we too have been captured by the spirit of neoliberalism. We regularly retreat into the world of individual action and neglect what we could do together, as a Society of Friends.

How might we revitalise our ability to act collectively as a Society in order to contribute to a just and sustainable peace? Yes, we have Regional Meetings, Yearly Meetings, Clearness Meetings, and far too many committees, many of which I would lay down in a heartbeat. The real question, I think, is: Do we truly want to act together as a whole Society? And if so, are our processes sufficient? What else might deepen and broaden the bonds that bind us, open us up more to those most affected, including other-than-human voices, and enable us to band together to let the Spirit act through us in concert? Are we ready to commit to truly doing something together before agreeing *what* that something might be?

This commitment to act together before deciding what to act on does not have to be complicated or foreign. It may be as simple as turning towards each other, knowing our own stories and having the skills to share our biographies in ways that are enlivened by our faith and practice. Could we listen to one another at a deeper level until we truly understand why we do what we do? Might we listen, not just once but habitually? What would it take for our Meetings to become deeper, so that we truly *meet* one another, knowing intimately what makes each one of us 'tick' and the eternal spirit within? Imagine if, in every Meeting, there were an ongoing preparation and organisation to help us know each other like that. As relationships form, we would naturally explore what keeps us awake at night, together discerning what may be a 'bother' or a concern and whether a leading is emerging, not just for a Meeting or Regional Meeting but for the whole Society. Such a listening and discernment process would need to be backed up by soft infrastructure: ongoing training and organisers ('elders') embraced by each Meeting, who are willing to support and guide the process. It would also need to be not only shaped but also actively led by those who are most affected by injustice, of whom a number are already connected to various Meetings. Perhaps some of you might say, 'We already do that'. But I think, 'not yet, Friends'. Sure, there are helpful practices, histories, hints, threads and promises, but we are not yet expressing our full potential to act collectively. We have a rich tradition and solid foundation to build on, but I want to suggest that we do not yet have the right structures and processes in place to support powerful nonviolent collective action. But we could nurture those structures and processes. Of course, perhaps I am mistaken. Perhaps, Meeting exists primarily to nourish and nurture individuals and their faith? There would be nothing wrong with that. That would be good. It *is* good. And yet…we are called a 'Society'. I don't think that is by coincidence f/Friends. What does it mean to truly *be* and *do* 'Society'?

The second point is related to the first. What would it take to combine faith *and* strategy, for one to naturally flow into the other? How do we become much more skilled at that? Forgive me for being blunt, Friends, but our faith sometimes looks like what Paulo Freire called 'magical thinking', believing that activities like vigils and letters are enough or that wishing for change will make it happen. But wishful thinking is not enough. I know of no single major change anywhere in the world that was the result of a single protest or action disconnected from persistent and escalating expressions of power. If we just share information, hold a vigil or write a letter, then somehow God, the Spirit, or whatever word we choose to use, will do the rest. At best, this is a dying gasp as we sink into irrelevance. Do we really want to act as co-creators with the Spirit to transform the world? If so, are we willing to invest in strategy—and movement-building skills—that are wedded to reorganising the Society as a unified voice in solidarity with the living earth and those on the margins? Are we willing to be co-led by young people as we do this?

Our Testimonies provide guidance, but I believe they need to be sharpened by a collective commitment to act, and by strategy skills focused on reclaiming the Commons and realising a 500-year-old vision of a nonviolent future—the 'good life', the 'beloved community', 'heaven on earth' if you like. Our Testimonies offer glimpses of this vision. My own hope is also grounded in my experience of accompanying Indigenous movements, which for me embody and point to a better world/s for all of us: humans and our other relations, mother earth, father sky.

In 1660, George Fox and a handful of other 'peculiar people' declared they wanted to take away the occasion for all wars. Friends, empire is war in a concentrated and permanent form. Dismantling empire should be our core business. Embarking on a decolonial journey towards 'the good life' is at the heart of Quaker faith and practice. In a country such as Australia, deep in denial about the frontier wars and the ongoing effects of colonialism, a shared commitment to animate freedom could be balm for our collective soul.

In accompanying the West Papuan freedom movement and other Indigenous movements for self-determination, I have heard George Fox speaking to us as a Society. It is an invitation to begin where we started: to make our faith and practice dangerous again. And to do that together. Is it a call to nonviolence? Absolutely! It is also a call to be disruptive and creative.

Thank you, Friends. Go well.

# References

Banks, Sarah. 2019. 'Ethics, Equity and Community Development: Mapping the Terrain'. In *Ethics, Equity and Community Development*, edited by Sarah Banks and Peter Westoby. Bristol, UK: Policy Press.

Brindle, Susannah Kay. 2000. *To Learn a New Song: A Quaker Contribution Towards Real Reconciliation with the Earth and its Peoples*. The James Backhouse Lectures. Australia: The Religious Society of Friends (Quakers).

Buber, Martin. 1937 (2009). *I and Thou*. Translated by Ronald Gregor Smith. The University of Michigan: T. and T. Clark. Digitised version.

Burrowes, Robert. 1996. *The Strategy of Nonviolent Defense: A Gandhian Approach*. Albany, NY: State University of New York Press.

Carline, David, supported by Cheryl Buchanan. 2017. *Reflections on the 50th Anniversary of the 1967 Referendum in the Context of Two Aboriginal Life Stories*. The James Backhouse Lectures. Australia: The Religious Society of Friends (Quakers).

Denborough, David. 2008. *Collective Narrative Practice: Responding to Individuals, Groups, and Communities Who Have Experienced Trauma*. Adelaide: Dulwich Centre Publications.

Engler, Mark, and Paul Engler. 2016. *This Is an Uprising: How Nonviolent Revolt is Shaping the Twenty-First Century*. New York: Nation Books.

Escobar, Arturo. 2017. *Designs for the Pluriverse: Radical Interdependence, Autonomy, and the Making of Worlds*. Durham and London: Duke University Press.

Fanon, Frantz. 1963. *The Wretched of the Earth*. New York: Grove.

Fanon, Frantz. 1965. *A Dying Colonialism*. New York: Grove.

Francis, Diane. 2002. *People, Peace and Power: Conflict Transformation in Action*. London: Pluto Press.

Freire, Paulo. (1968) 1972. *Pedagogy of the Oppressed*. London and New York: Penguin Books.

Gandhi, Mohandas K. 1909. *Hind Swaraj or Indian Home Rule*. Ahmedabad: Navajivan.

Gandhi, Mohandas K. 1945. *Constructive Programme: Its Meaning and Place*. Ahmedabad: Navajivan.

Ganz, Marshall. 2009. *Why David Sometimes Wins: Leadership, Strategy and the Organization in the California Farm Worker Movement*. Oxford: Oxford University Press.

Gaventa, John. 2006. 'Finding the Spaces for Change: A Power Analysis'. *IDS Bulletin*, 37 (6): 23–33.

Gecan, Michael. 2004. *Going Public: An Organizer's Guide to Citizen Action*. New York: Anchor Books.

Giay, Benny. 2000. *Menuju Papua Baru: Beberapa Pokok Pikiran Sekitar Emansipasi Orang Papua*. Paniai and Jayapura: Deiyei and ELSHAM.

Horton, Myles, and Paulo Freire. 1990. *We Make the Road by Walking: Conversations on Education and Social Change*. Philadelphia: Temple University Press.

James, David, and Jillian Wychel. 1991. *Loving the Distances Between: Racism, Culture and Spirituality*. The James Backhouse Lectures. Australia: The Religious Society of Friends (Quakers).

Johnstone, Chris, and Joanna Macy. 2012. *Active Hope: How to Face the Mess We're in Without Going Crazy*. Australia and New Zealand: Finch Publishing.

Kelly, Anthony, and Peter Westoby. 2018. *Participatory Development Practice: Using Traditional and Contemporary Frameworks*. Rugby, UK: Practical Action Publishing.

Land, Clare. 2015. *Decolonising Solidarity: Dilemmas and Directions for Supporters of Indigenous Struggles*. London: Zed Books.

Lakey, George. 2001. *The Sword That Heals*. Philadelphia: Training for Change.

Lakey, George. 2010. *Facilitating Group Learning: Strategies for Success with Adult Learners*. San Francisco: Jossey-Bass.

Lakey, George. 2018. *How We Win: A Guide to Nonviolent Direct Action*

*Campaigning*. New York: Random House.

Lederach, John Paul. 1995. *Preparing for Peace: Conflict Transformation across Cultures.* New York: Syracuse University Press.

Lukes, Steven. 1974. *Power: A Radical View.* London: Macmillan (reprinted 2004, Basingstoke: Palgrave Macmillan)

MacLeod, Jason. 2013. 'West Papua: Civil Resistance, Framing, and Identity 1910s–2012'. In *Recovering Nonviolent History: Civil Resistance beneath Eulogized Violence,* edited by Maciej J. Bartkowski. Boulder, Colorado: Lynne Reiner Publishers.

MacLeod, Jason. 2015. *Civil Resistance in West Papua: Merdeka and the Morning Star.* Brisbane: University of Queensland Press.

MacLeod, Jason, and James Whelan. 2015. *People Power Manual: Campaign Strategy.* Inala: Pasifika and The Change Agency.

McAllister, Pam. 1988. *You Can't Kill the Spirit.* Santa Cruz: New Society Publishers.

McIntosh, Alastair. 2001. *Soil and Soul: People versus Corporate Power.* London: Aurum Press.

McIntosh, Alastair. 2016. *Poacher's Pilgrimage: An Island Journey.* Edinburgh: Birlinn.

Mindell, Arnold. 1995. *Sitting in the Fire: Large Group Transformation Using Conflict and Diversity.* Portland: Lao Tse Press.

Pittock, Barrie. 1969. *Toward a Multi-Racial Society.* The James Backhouse Lectures. Australia: The Religious Society of Friends.

Scheiner, Charles. 2006. *Self-Determination Requires More Than Political Independence: Recent Developments in Timor-Leste.* Dili: La'o Hamutuk.

Scott, James C. 1990. *Domination and the Arts of Resistance: Hidden Transcripts.* New Haven: Yale University Press.

Sennett, Richard. 2002. *Respect in a World of Inequality.* London: Penguin.

Smith, Linda Tuhiwai. 1999. *Decolonizing Methodologies: Research and Indigenous Peoples.* London: Zed Books and University of Otago Press.

Stiehm, Judith. 1968. 'Nonviolence Is Two.' *Sociological Inquiry* 38 (1): 23–30.

Vinthagen, Stellan. 2015. *A Theory of Nonviolent Action: How Civil Resistance Works.* London: Zed Books.

Walker, Polly O. (Daksi). 2006. *One Heart and a Wrong Spirit: The Religious Society of Friends and Colonial Racism.* The James Backhouse Lectures. Australia: The Religious Society of Friends (Quakers).

Wright, Erik Olin. 2010. *Envisioning Real Utopias.* London: Verso.

www.ingramcontent.com/pod-product-compliance
Lightning Source LLC
Chambersburg PA
CBHW070931280326
41934CB00009B/1830